FACTS ON FILE SCIENCE SOURCEBOOKS

TALKING BONES
THE SCIENCE OF
FORENSIC ANTHROPOLOGY

PEGGY THOMAS

Facts On File, Inc.

For Francis

Talking Bones: The Science of Forensic Anthropology

Facts On File, Inc.
11 Penn Plaza
New York NY 10001

Library of Congress Cataloging-in-Publication Data

Thomas, Peggy.
    Talking bones : the science of forensic anthropology / Peggy Thomas.
        p.   cm. — (Facts On File science sourcebooks)
    Includes bibliographical references and index.
    Summary: Introduces the history, technology, and importance of the science of using human remains to solve crimes and includes actual forensic cases.
    ISBN 0-8160-3114-2
    1. Forensic anthropology—Juvenile literature. 2. Forensic osteology—Juvenile literature.   [1. Forensic anthropology.]
    I. Title. II. Series
    GN69.8.T48   1995
    614′.1—dc20   94–44110

Facts On File books are available at special discounts when purchased in bulk quantities for businesses, associations, institutions, or sales promotions. Please call our Special Sales Department in New York at 212/967-8800 or 800/322-8755.

You can find Facts On File on the World Wide Web at http://www.factsonfile.com

Text design by Catherine Rincon Hyman
Cover design by Amy Gonzalez
Illustrations by Marc Greene
On the cover: William Maples of the C. A. Pound Human ID Laboratory of the Florida Museum of Natural History at the University of Florida.

Printed in the United States of America

MP FOF 10 9 8 7 6 5 4 3

This book is printed on acid-free paper.

Contents

Acknowledgments   vi

Diagram of the Human Skeleton   vii

Diagram of the Human Skull   viii

1 The Butcher and the Doctor   1
The Parkman Murder   5

2 Building a Science   9
Forensic Sciences   10
Partners in Crime   11
War and Research   13

3 Is It Human?   16
The Humerus of a Human Compared to That of Various Animals   17
Cross sections of Human and Nonhuman Bone   18
Hands and Paws   19
Horse Tails and Dog Bones   21

4 The Scene of the Crime   23
Buried Bones   26
Natural Disasters   28
The Forensic Response Team   29

5 The Body Farm   31
Rate of Decay   34

Sight, Smell, Touch		36
The Bug Detective		37
The Lifecycle of the Blowfly		38
Underwater Insects		41

6 Hidden Identity   42

Male or Female?	42
Skeletal Differences of the Male and Female Pelvis	43
Skeletal Differences of the Male and Female Skull	45
Age at Death	47
Epiphysial Ossification	48
The Eruption Sequence of the Permanent Teeth	50
Race	51
The Pencil Test	53
Stature	54

7 We Are What We Do   56

Occupational Trauma	57
Handedness	58
Disease and Illness	60
Positive Identification	62
Genetic Fingerprinting	63
Making a DNA Print	64

8 Weapons, Wounds, and Cause of Death   66

Old Murders	67
Chicken Legs and Finger Bones	68
Rodents' Chew Markings	70
Weapons	70
Distinctive Wounds Caused by Tools	71
Burned Bones	73
The Case of the Body in the Burned Out Car	74

9 Face Finding   77

Reconstruction	78
Finding Frank	79
Science and Art	82

Grinner—A Face from the Past 83
The Reconstruction of Grinner 84

10 Photographic Superimposition 90
Case of the Missing Prison Guard 92
Mitch Boyer 93
Bones, Bullets, and Bank Robbers 95

11 Graveyard Detectives 97
Graveyard Detectives 101
On the Outlaw Trail 103

12 Old Bones 107
Non-invasive Analysis 108
Trace Elements 109
Family Ties 111
Ancient Disease 111
Wounds of War 113
Native American Remains 114
The Body in the Bog 115
African Burial Ground 116
Lone Survivor 118

13 Giving Voice to the Victims 121
Argentina 121
Hungary 124
Casualties of War 126
The Homeless 127
Silent Witness 128
The Future 129

Glossary 130

Further Reading 132

Index 133

ACKNOWLEDGMENTS

I would like to thank all the people who shared their expertise and anecdotes with me. Their enthusiasm for forensic anthropology was catching, and I thoroughly enjoyed even the most morbid details. Thank you to Michael Finnegan, professor at Kansas State University; William Maples at the C.A. Pound Human ID Lab at the University of Florida; William M. Bass at the University of Tennessee; Douglas H. Ubelaker and David Hunt at the Smithsonian Institution; Jeffery Barnes, forensic entomologist at the New York State Museum; Dael Morris at the Royal Ontario Museum. And a special thanks to Kathleen Arries, forensic anthropologist and associate professor at Erie Community College, who opened up her home and file cabinets to me, and explained everything so simply. Thank you to Marilyn Greenwell at the Middleport Free Library for locating research materials, and to my first draft readers Fran Thomas, Margery, and Howard Facklam.

HUMAN SKELETON

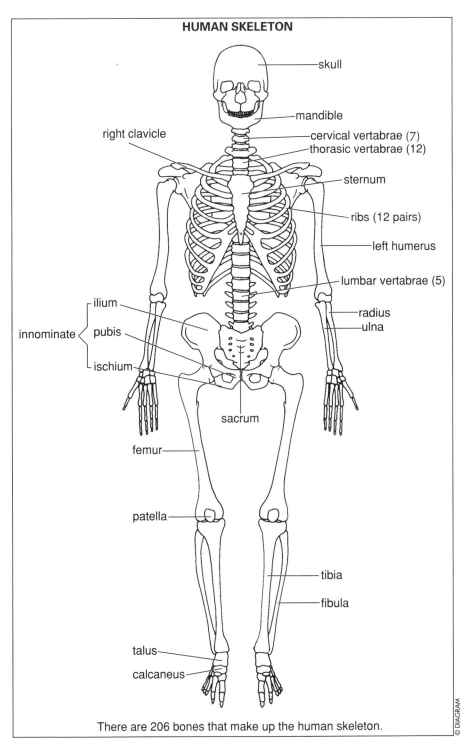

- skull
- mandible
- cervical vertabrae (7)
- thorasic vertabrae (12)
- sternum
- ribs (12 pairs)
- left humerus
- lumbar vertabrae (5)
- radius
- ulna
- right clavicle
- ilium
- innominate
- pubis
- ischium
- sacrum
- femur
- patella
- tibia
- fibula
- talus
- calcaneus

There are 206 bones that make up the human skeleton.

© DIAGRAM

HUMAN SKULL

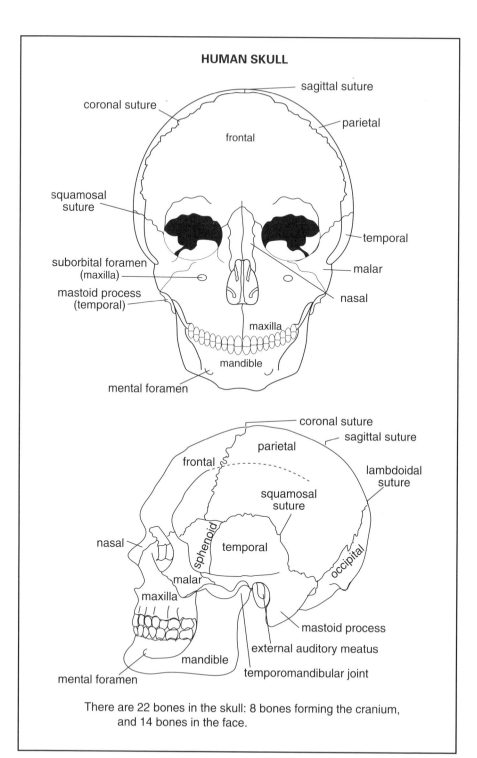

There are 22 bones in the skull: 8 bones forming the cranium, and 14 bones in the face.

THE BUTCHER
AND THE DOCTOR

*O*ld man Luetgert made sausage from his wife.
He turned up the steam.
She began to scream.
There'll be a hot time in the old town tonight.

In 1897, along the streets of Chicago you could hear children skipping rope to this morbid refrain as the trial of Adolphe Luetgert filled the front pages of the local newspapers.

Adolphe Luetgert was a well known sausage maker in Chicago, and when his wife Louisa mysteriously disappeared, he claimed that she had run off to relatives after an argument. But the neighbors became suspicious when Luetgert's two young sons began to ask door to door if anyone had seen their mother. Six days later, in order to stop the rumors, Luetgert finally reported Louisa's disappearance to the police.

Police Captain Herman Schuettler and a team of officers interviewed people in the neighborhood who described Luetgert as a wife beater and adulterer. Luetgert did not even live in the house with his family but slept in a back office of the sausage factory next door. Business associates told police about Luetgert's ambitious attempts to increase his sausage-making business, even though his wife disapproved.

Schuettler suspected Luetgert of murder, but he needed evidence against him. Police questioned the workers in the sausage factory who informed them that weeks before the disappearance of his wife, Luetgert made an unusual order of 375 pounds of potash and 50 pounds of arsenic to be delivered to the factory.

The night guard told the police that on the night of the disappearance Luetgert sent him on an errand and then gave him the rest of the night off. The guard left Luetgert in the sausage factory, stirring a boiling liquid in a huge cooking vat. The guard had never seen his employer do that before, and according to the other employees Luetgert fired up the furnace under the vat and kept vigil all night and the next day.

Witnesses claimed they saw Luetgert and his wife entering the factory late in the evening, and others swore they heard screams coming from inside the building. Schuettler ordered his men to search the factory; to look inside crates, under machinery, and inside the cooking vats. The vat Luetgert had personally kept boiling that infamous night was drained through a spigot at its base as officers sat around the foul smelling sludge, poking through it with wooden sticks. And in the putrid slime they found the evidence, a small bone, a ring guard, and a wedding ring with the engraving L. L. on the inside. A further search of the ashes outside the building uncovered a bone hairpin, a steel corset stay, several bone fragments, and a false tooth.

Experts from the University of Chicago reported to the police that boiling potash and arsenic would have dissolved a human body within two hours. Based on all this evidence, Luetgert was arrested for the murder of his wife.

George Dorsey was the first anthropologist to testify in court regarding the identity of bones found at a crime scene. (The Field Museum, Neg#A108072, Chicago)

Adolphe may have cooked his wife, but the rumor spread that he made sausage from her too. The more the children sang, the more sausage sales dropped in the Chicago area.

Charles Deneen, the Illinois State's Attorney was assigned to prosecute at the trial, but he had a problem. How could he prove a murder actually took place without having a body to prove it? At the trial Deneen called Luetgert "one of the most dastardly murderers in history," "an inhuman fiend" who sat and watched his wife sink into the boiling vat, but Luetgert's defense attorney produced witnesses who claimed they saw Louisa at a railroad station 50 miles away. The jury was confused and deadlocked. The judge dismissed them and called for another jury.

A second trial was prepared with a new jury, but the prosecutor was still having difficulty proving murder. To Deneen's dismay, Dr.

Walter H. Allport of the Chicago Medical College, who was called to testify, declared that the remains "may be human, but just as likely they may be from some lower animal."

Needing real expertise to win this case, Prosecutor Deneen called on George Dorsey, a *physical anthropologist* at the Field Museum of Natural History in Chicago, whose specialty was the study of ancient human remains. Dorsey had spent his career researching how to determine sex from a skeleton. This case was right up his alley.

After examining the bone fragments, Dorsey testified, "I have found no bones from the hog, dog or sheep which have any of the characteristics which distinguish these bones. In my judgment, they belong to one human body." He also testified that the small bone found in the vat was the sesamoid bone from the joint of the big toe. The sesamoid, named because it resembles a sesame seed, is embedded in the tendons of the toe and acts as a ball bearing that helps the human foot to bend.

A columnist for the *Chicago Tribune* observed Dorsey in the courtroom and was impressed with what he saw:

His knowledge was so well systematized, so well in hand, so sound, precise and broad, that it was a pleasure to listen to him: it is not often one comes in contact with a brain of so fine a fiber, so vigorous, and so sane.

Dorsey's testimony bolstered the already damaging evidence against Luetgert, and the case was closed. Luetgert was convicted and sentenced to life in prison.

The Luetgert trial was the first time an anthropologist took the witness stand in a *forensic* case. Forensics is a legal argument. It was clear that a physical anthropologist, who studies the human body and how groups of humans differ physically, might know more about human bones than a medical doctor. Unfortunately, Dorsey found out the difficulties of breaking into forensic work. His academic career suffered when colleagues complained that he had "lowered" himself by "performing" at a trial, and others could not

∇

believe that he had the nerve to challenge the testimony of a medical doctor. Because of this, Dorsey dropped his forensic pursuits and joined the navy.

But Dorsey's testimony opened the door for other anthropologists who until then had only consulted for law enforcement quietly in their labs. The methodology Dorsey used to determine that the bones in the vat were the remains of Louisa Luetgert had already been established in court only a short time before in another grisly murder trial.

The Parkman Murder

The Friday before Thanksgiving, 1849, Dr. George Parkman walked through Boston, Massachusetts as he did every day, running

$3,000 REWARD!

DR. GEORGE PARKMAN,

A well known citizen of Boston, left his residence No. 8 Walnut Street, on Friday last, he is 60 years of age ;—about 5 feet 9 inches high—grey hair—thin face— with a scar under his chin—light complexion—and usually walks very fast. He was dressed in a dark frock coat, dark pantaloons, purple silk vest, with dark figured black stock and black hat.

As he may have wandered from home in consequence of some sudden aberration of mind, being perfectly well when he left his house; or, as he had with him a large sum of money, he may have been foully dealt with. The above reward will be paid for information which will lead to his discovery if alive; or for the detection and conviction of the perpetrators if any injury may have been done to him. A suitable reward will be paid for the discovery of his body.

Boston, Nov. 26th, 1849. **ROBERT G. SHAW.**

Information may be given to the City Marshal.

From the Congress Printing House,(Farwell & Co.) 32 Congress St.

Twenty-eight thousand handbills were posted throughout Boston in an attempt to get information about Parkman's whereabouts. (Massachusetts Historical Society)

errands and visiting patients. He was a prominent physician and a wealthy man noted for his land dealings. On this particular Friday, he was on his way to the Parkman Medical Building at the Harvard Medical School, named after him because he had donated the land on which it was built. On the way he stopped to buy a head of lettuce from the local grocer, leaving it there to be picked up when he returned.

At the medical school, Parkman met with another prominent physician and professor, Dr. John Webster, who was noted for enjoying life. An avid gambler, Webster had borrowed heavily from Parkman to cover debts, and it was this debt that Parkman was coming to collect. According to Webster, he and Parkman had a pleasant conversation, and he paid his debt willingly. After Parkman received the money he left, and Webster claimed he never saw him again.

Parkman never picked up the lettuce, and he never returned home. His brother-in-law called the police and later posted 28,000 handbills across the city offering a $3,000 reward for information of Parkman's whereabouts.

The police questioned the amiable Webster about his meeting with Parkman and took his statement, but they did not suspect Webster of murder. In fact, they were not convinced there had been any foul play at all.

The janitor at the medical school, Ephraim Littlefield, on the other hand, was very suspicious. He claimed that Webster had been acting unusually kind, giving Littlefield the week off, and sending a Thanksgiving turkey to his home.

Littlefield roamed every inch of the medical building he knew so well, looking for evidence. He did not find anything until he went into the basement, which was made up of several chambers or pits that collected sewage and debris from the rooms above. These pits then emptied into the river, which carried the foul smells and gunk away.

As Littlefield later told the jury, on a hunch he went to the stone pit that sat underneath Webster's office and latrine. With his wife holding a lantern above him, Littlefield used a pick axe to break through the stone wall. In the dim light he peered in, and there he saw a hacked up body hanging on a hook similar to the ones used to hold cadavers in the medical school upstairs. In the dirt and slime at the bottom of the pit, he found the remains of a pelvis.

The police found the rest. Searching through Webster's office they found the rib section in a tea chest, a set of false teeth in the oven, and burned bone and a button in the furnace. It appeared that Parkman was all over the place. Webster was arrested that evening and taken to jail.

A team of doctors from the Harvard Medical College were called in to examine and identify the remains. The team included Jefferies Wyman, an anatomist at the college; a dentist, Nathan Keep; and Oliver Wendell Holmes, dean of the Medical College, an anatomist (and father of the younger Oliver Wendell Holmes who would grow up to be a justice on the United States Supreme Court). First, the team toured the scene of the crime, inspecting where the remains were found. The 150-odd bones collected from the medical building were then laid out and examined. It was Wyman's job to reassemble them in anatomical order. The team agreed that they were indeed human remains because of the shape of the pelvis and teeth. They proceeded to identify the remains as those from a male 50 to 60 years old, and 5 feet, 10 inches tall. Parkman was 60 years old when he died and had stood 5 feet 11 inches.

Nathan Keep was on the team because he was Parkman's dentist and had given Parkman a set of false teeth made specially to fit the jutting, prominent jaw, which had earned Parkman the nickname "Chin." Dr. Keep examined the charred and battered false teeth and testified that this set found in Webster's oven was the same set he had made for Parkman. He showed the jurors the unusual shape of the denture plate that would fit only Parkman.

When the trial opened on March 19, 1850, it was the biggest show in town, with the bones as the star witness. With the help of the doctors and the dentist, the prosecutor was able to convince the jury to bring in a guilty verdict, and Webster was sentenced to hang.

More than a century later, historians have raised questions about Webster's guilt, based on mishandling of the trial. Some researchers have questioned whether the remains truly were Parkman's or whether they were planted by an unscrupulous Littlefield to get the $3,000 reward. We may never know.

Nevertheless, the Webster trial set the standard procedure for identifying bones that every forensic anthropologist uses today, which must answer a series of ten questions.

1. Are the bones human?
2. How many individuals are represented?
3. How long ago did death occur?
4. What was the person's age at death?
5. What was the person's sex?
6. What was the person's race?
7. What was the person's height?
8. Are there any identifying characteristics, such as old injuries, disease, or unusual features (such as Parkman's chin)?
9. What was the cause of death?
10. What was the manner of death (homicide, suicide, accidental, natural, or unknown)?

Before the sensational cases of Webster and Luetgert, detective work was done only by the police. Science played a small role in solving crime, and bone analysis was rarely used, but as cities grew bigger and crime more prevalent the police turned to science for help.

2

BUILDING A SCIENCE

*I*n the United States, there is a legal procedure for handling dead bodies. If the manner of death is unknown or suspect, the coroner or medical examiner is called in to perform an autopsy to determine cause of death, but this was not always the case.

Originally the coroner was a tax collector for the king of England in the 18th century. When a person died, his or her family was required to pay a tax, and the coroner arrived at the death scene to see that the family paid up. Even after the death tax was abolished, the coroner still showed up when a person died to help solve any disputes as to the cause of death. Those coroners had no medical training, and this system lasted for centuries.

In the early 1900s New York State had a wide assortment of unqualified men who held the job of coroner, including eight undertakers, seven politicians, six real estate agents, two bar owners, two barbers, one butcher, and one milkman. Perhaps the most qualified were the undertakers and maybe the butcher. Although most states today have trained medical examiners, some still hire unqualified people such as morticians and tow truck operators whose primary qualification for the job is being able to haul the body away. So it is easy to see why some people get away with murder.

Forensic Sciences

A science that is used to solve crime is called a forensic science. Science began to make its mark in the forensic field in the 1800s with the onset of forensic ballistics, which is matching bullet marks to the guns that fired them; forensic toxicology, which is the science of detecting poison in the body; and fingerprinting. These procedures were not practiced regularly, but selectively by specialists who were just developing them.

The science of bone study was slower to grasp the forensic world. A dead body was not considered a source of evidence, and if a body had decomposed until there was nothing left but bones, most detectives felt it was useless even to look at it.

In the late 1800s, European detectives were using a new technique of measuring the human body in order to recognize and catch criminals. It was called *anthropometry.*

Cesare Lombroso, an Italian physician, measured convicts and developed a list of the physical characteristics that he considered typical of a criminal man: large jaw, heavy brow, large deep set eyes, high cheekbones, handle-shaped ears, and a thick skull. Although this idea seemed based in science, it didn't work. According to this principle, no matter how law-abiding a man was, if he fit the description, he could be mistaken for a criminal and hanged.

Alphonse Bertillon, a French police clerk, expanded on Lombroso's work and developed the anthropometric "print" based on the theory that no two men could have the exact same body measurements. He made a list of 11 measurements for every arrested criminal to go along with their mug shot. The list included facial and body measurements, height, gait (the way someone walks), and dress. The list, however, was cumbersome and lengthy and was soon replaced with a better system.

Fingerprinting, a technique that Bertillon had experimented with but abandoned, was also being developed by the English, and at the same time by an Argentine police officer named Juan Vucetich, who, in 1892, was the first person known to solve a case using fingerprinting. Two children had been found dead in a small village of Necochea. The mother accused her boyfriend of killing them, but the boyfriend had an airtight alibi. The police suspected the mother of killing the children in a rage, but had no proof until Vucetich lifted a bloody thumbprint from the door frame of the family's house. It matched the mother's print exactly. When she was confronted with the evidence, she confessed.

Fingerprinting proved to be more manageable and more accurate than anthropometric prints, and it was widely adopted by law enforcement agencies around the world.

In the United States, anthropometry was seldom used by the police, but it was used extensively in the academic field. While Bertillon was measuring criminals in France, Thomas Dwight was measuring cadavers at Harvard University. Dr. Dwight had the idea that the bones of the human body reflected the various traits of the individual. He focused on groups of humans and how they differed physically from each other, which is the focus of physical anthropology itself. Dwight was successful in proving that a bone expert could measure a single bone and "read" various conclusions from it about a person's height, sex, and age and write an "osteobiography," a skeletal history of that person's life. Some in the field today credit Dwight as the father of forensic anthropology.

Forensic anthropology developed and became more acceptable as anthropologists, eager to practice their craft, assisted police departments that needed better technology to solve murders.

Partners in Crime

The National Museum of Natural History at the Smithsonian Institution in Washington, D.C. has one of the finest *anthropology* departments in the country. Its long hallways are lined with tall cupboards filled with more than 33,000 skeletons that make up one of the largest human skeletal reference collections in the world.

In the 1930s the Smithsonian got a new neighbor when the Federal Bureau of Investigation (FBI) moved in across the street, and like all good neighbors they helped each other. FBI agents

The Smithsonian Institution's 33,000 skeletons compose one of the largest skeletal collections in the world. (Physical Anthropology Division of the Deptartment of Anthropology, National Museum of Natural History)

would lug body parts over to the museum to be examined by the academically minded anthropologists.

Although anthropologists examined bones for the police now and then, it was never considered appropriate behavior, and the practice was seldom discussed or written about until Wilton M. Krogman, a physical anthropologist at Case Western Reserve Medical School, wrote the "Guide to the Identification of Human Skeletal Material" for the *FBI Law Enforcement Bulletin*. This one article let forensic anthropology out of the closet. Because the article was published in the 1930s during the violent years of the gangster era, the FBI began to see how useful bone experts could be in solving murder cases. More and more frequently they called on the curator of anthropology at the Smithsonian, Dale Stewart, to examine bodies and bones. Stewart formalized the relationship between the FBI and the Smithsonian and trained two generations of scientists and FBI agents. In 1979 he wrote the first textbook for forensic anthropology.

Today, Douglas Ubelaker, the current curator of anthropology at the Smithsonian, serves as chief consultant for the FBI. He divides his time between his academic research on Mesoamerican Indians and the 40 or so forensic cases that are sent over from the FBI each year. Ubelaker works closely with FBI special agent Robert Fram from the hair and fiber division and together they identify bodies that come to the FBI from all over the country. If odd bones are picked up by someone walking through the woods, for example (and this does happen, as Ubelaker explains), Ubelaker can tell whether the remains are human or animal. Along with others in the anthropology department, Ubelaker also aids the FBI by creating clay reconstructions of a person's face, superimposing portraits with skulls and conducting microscopic analysis.

War and Research

It is hard to do research in forensic anthropology because you need human bodies to study, and lots of them. Before the 1940s most of

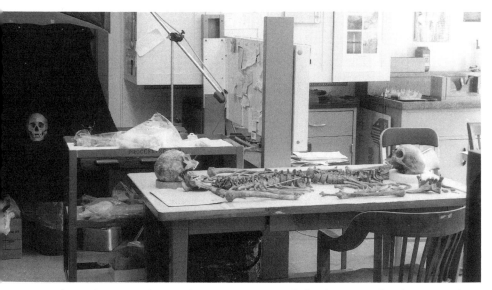

Anthropologists at the Smithsonian examine skeletal remains for the FBI and other law enforcement agencies around the country. (Physical Anthropology Division of the Department of Anthropology, National Museum of Natural History)

the information about sex, race, age, and stature came from skeletons excavated from archaeological sites or from unknown bodies called John or Jane Does at the morgue. In the early half of this century, the most widely used means of determining stature was based on an early French study that consisted of only 12 patients from an insane asylum. A dozen homeless and insane patients do not provide accurate data. (For scientific studies to be considered valid, they need to be based on large numbers of individuals.)

For accurate results, a study should include bodies that are well-documented with the known age at death, as well as the height and health of the person. The end of World War II offered the first

Unpacking bones for examination. The ribs are counted and every fragment is inventoried. (Kathleen O. Arries)

major opportunity to study large numbers of well-documented bodies because every soldier had a complete and accurate health record. One hour of battle during WWII supplied more than enough bodies for years of research. Anthropologists were hired by the U.S. Army to help *repatriate* the war dead, which meant identifying the bodies and returning them to their home countries. Mildred Trotter, professor of gross anatomy at Washington University, St. Louis and a physical anthropologist, was assigned to head up the lab in Hawaii charged with identifying the dead from some of the worst battles in the Pacific, including those that took place on Iwo Jima, on Guadalcanal, and in the Philippines. She was the first woman to hold this position. Many of the bodies brought into the lab had no identifying characteristics, and it was her job to examine the bones and come up with an identification based on X rays, dental charts, and health records supplied by the army and relatives of the deceased.

While working on the identification of the war dead, Dr. Trotter persuaded the army to let her measure the dead and collect data that would later become the standards that forensic anthropologists use today to estimate height from bones.

In the 1950s more data was collected from similar repatriation efforts after the Korean War. On assignment for the U.S. Army, anthropologist Dale Stewart and his men worked for four months in a smelly warehouse on the Japanese island of Kyushu surrounded by stacked boxes full of the bones of American soldiers. Stewart's research resulted in the method used today to estimate a skeleton's age at death. It is based on the amount of bone growth between the knobby ends of the *long bones* and the shaft of the long bones.

The repatriation program trained many physical anthropologists with the skills to become forensic experts, and in 1970, with the formation of the American Association of Forensic Anthropology, a program was developed to certify these experts. It is a small group with exclusive membership for those who have a keen eye for spotting the subtle differences between male and female skulls, a sharp mind to decipher the clues, and a strong stomach for gruesome and grisly murder.

3

IS IT HUMAN?

*W*hen all that remains of a person are small bits of bone sealed in a Zip-lock bag, the first question that the forensic anthropologist asks is "Is it human?" Human bones that are whole and *articulated* (still attached to each other) are easy to identify, but when bones are broken or burned, and the *epiphyses* (the bony caps of the long bones) have been chewed off by wild animals or cut off by a murderer, the job of identifying them gets more difficult.

When Lawrence Angel was curator of anthropology at the National Museum of Natural History at the Smithsonian Institution in Washington, D.C. he estimated that 10 to 15 percent of all bones that are presumed to be human are really animal. Weeding out that 10 to 15 percent saves taxpayers money and the police hours of tedious investigation.

"Is it human?" is a legal question. Every human bone that is found must be investigated as thoroughly as possible. A civil case of accidental or natural death affects insurance claims, wills, and the financial matters of the deceased and his or her family. A criminal case could result in the capture and conviction of a murderer or even a serial killer.

Kathleen O. Arries, an associate professor of biology at Erie Community College and forensic anthropologist on the sheriff's department's scientific staff in Erie County, New York, says that when a bone comes in from the police department she just has to "eyeball it," but eyeballing in forensics means she has to know her bones, both human and animal. Expertise in both human and animal anatomy is one of the important and unusual strengths of the forensic anthropologist.

At a glance, Arries may notice that the rib bone is too large or the skull fragment is too thick to be human. She then compares the unknown bones to her reference collection, which is a set of skeletons of animals common to the area. Arries's collection consists of road kills, dead animals found in the woods, and donations from her local butcher. Each skeleton is cleaned and set out to bleach on her

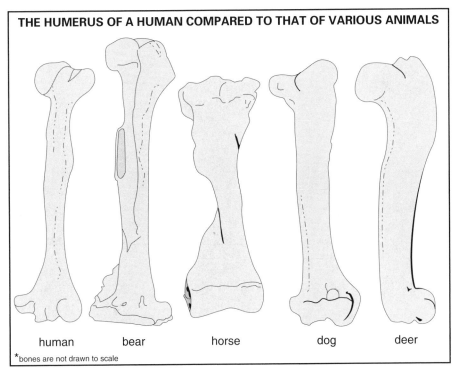

THE HUMERUS OF A HUMAN COMPARED TO THAT OF VARIOUS ANIMALS

human   bear   horse   dog   deer

*bones are not drawn to scale

Figure 1 This diagram shows the humerus of a human compared to those of a horse, bear, dog, and deer. Bones out of context are hard to identify. Comparing them to similar bones from other species shows how different the human anatomy is.

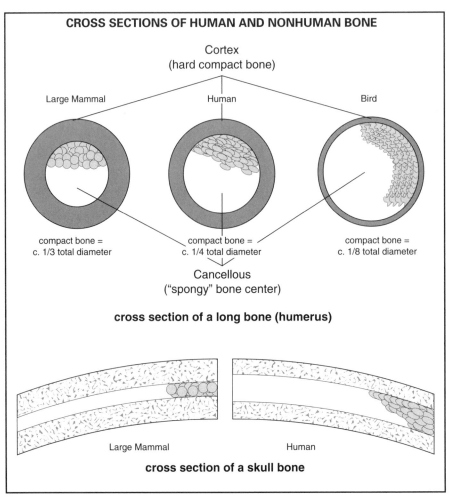

CROSS SECTIONS OF HUMAN AND NONHUMAN BONE

Cortex
(hard compact bone)

Large Mammal   Human   Bird

compact bone =   compact bone =   compact bone =
c. 1/3 total diameter c. 1/4 total diameter   c. 1/8 total diameter

Cancellous
("spongy" bone center)

cross section of a long bone (humerus)

Large Mammal   Human
cross section of a skull bone

Figure 2 The thickness of the bone is one way to tell if it is animal or human. In a large mammal the cortex is one-third the total diameter. In humans it is one-fourth the total diameter, and in birds the cortex is only one-eighth the total diameter of the bone.

back porch. If the suspect bone is not matched to one in her collection, she consults other specialists such as an ornithologist (someone who studies birds) or a mammologist (someone who studies mammals).

If Arries thinks that a bone, such as a fragment from a skull, may be human, she may try to fit the bone to a human reference skull, trying to match the contours of the bone fragment with those on the complete skull. If there are many fragments, she first must piece them together like a three-dimensional jigsaw puzzle.

The epiphyses of the long bones are good indicators of human-ness because of the angle of the joint. Our leg bones are attached to the pelvis at an angle to allow us to walk upright on two legs, unlike animals that walk on all fours. If the epiphyses have been broken off and only the shaft of the bone, called the *diaphysis*, is left, then a close look at the inside of the bone will give a clue as to what kind of animal it came from.

Bone is not solid but has a dense and hard outer layer with a spongy interior. The thickness of the outer layer, called the *cortex*, compared to the thickness of the total bone can indicate whether a bone is human or animal. In an adult human, the cortex is roughly one-fourth the total thickness of bone. Large mammals such as a dog or bear have a thicker cortex. It is one-third the total diameter. Birds have thin bones. The cortex of a bird is only one-eighth the total diameter of the bone.

Inside living bone there is a spongy material called cancellous tissue. Within this tissue are *osteons*, which are round tunnels that hold blood vessels and nerve fibers and carry nourishment to the surrounding bone. In humans, osteons are scattered randomly throughout the tissue. But in most animals the osteons are lined up in rows, so that a cross section under the microscope looks like a stack of bricks.

Many times, the circumstances in which suspect bones are found are more important than the bones themselves. We are all used to seeing chicken bones on our dinner plate, but we would think twice if we saw them poking out from under our neighbor's new rosebush. In a forensic context, many animal bones are mistaken for human remains.

Hands and Paws

In Colorado Springs, a dog happily gnawed on a bone, until the dog's owner, annoyed that his dog had gotten into someone's trash again, went to take the bone away. As the owner got closer, he saw that the dog was chewing on what looked like a human foot. The man called the police to investigate. It was indeed a foot, but there was no soft tissue left, and the last row of *phalanges* (finger and toe bones) were missing. It was hard to tell what kind of animal this foot had come from. The foot made the rounds at the local hospital, but no doctor was certain enough to say whether it was human or not. That evening the police launched a full-scale search for the rest of the body throughout the neighborhood.

Forensic anthropologist Michael Hoffman arrived the next morning to examine the bones. He saw that the foot was short, with no arch, and was missing not just one row of phalanges but two. He concluded that the foot was from a black bear, and the search for a murder victim was ended.

When a bear is skinned, the claws are removed by cutting off the first and sometimes the second row of phalanges, which shortens the feet, making them look remarkably like human hands and feet. But bears do not have opposable thumbs that can move and grasp. In anatomical position, which for humans is laying on the back with arms down at the sides, the hands are palms up. The anatomical position of a bear is standing up; paws are palms down. When positioned this way, the smallest digit of a bear paw is on the inside of the paw where our thumb is. This makes the bear paw a mirror image of human hands and feet. The right paw of a bear looks like the left hand and foot of a human.

The case of the mistaken bear paw has been repeated more than once throughout the country. One case in Hamburg, New York involved more than one foot. Two women out for a morning walk

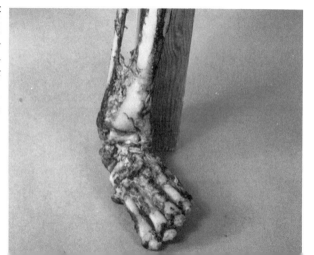

The skeletal left foot of a bear that has had its claws stripped away looks remarkably like the right foot of a human.
(Kathleen O. Arries)

through a cemetery noticed a severed foot lying in the road. A search of the surrounding woods turned up eight more severed feet. The cemetery was cordoned off and the badly decomposed feet were sent to a medical examiner who, without the skull or long bones, could not tell right away whether the remains were human or animal.

An anthropologist arrived on the scene and produced skeletal models of a human male foot and a human female foot from the trunk of her car. By comparing the severed feet to her reference skeletons, she could tell that they were not human. Later in the lab, she determined they were from four different black bears, three immature and one adult. A local taxidermist was called in for questioning about the illegal shooting of a mother bear and her cubs.

Another case involving mystery bones dug from someone's backyard baffled two orthopedic surgeons, but the forensic anthropologist who examined them knew immediately that the charred bones along with a number of ribs and sacrum (lower vertebrae) were part of an animal's tail. There was no murder victim, just the leftovers of a pig roast.

Medical doctors and medical examiners are trained to deal with the human body fully fleshed, and they rarely see random, loose bones of other animals. Forensic anthropologists see all kinds of animal bones frequently, even so, under some circumstances professional anthropologists can be fooled too.

Horse Tails and Dog Bones

Dale Stewart was working at the Smithsonian when he received a small package of bones from the FBI. They were labeled finger bones, and Stewart without questioning the label agreed. As he was examining them, he became puzzled about something. What animal did they come from? He sent them to a mammologist who determined that the bones came from a horse. They were not finger bones at all, but the tail bones of a horse.

The vertebrae in a horse's tail are similar in size and shape to human phalanges, with one subtle difference. The ends of the vertebrae are flat and sharp edged, whereas human finger bones are rounded at the top and bottom.

Knowing too much about a case can alter the way a specimen is examined, as Stewart found out by assuming the bones were finger bones instead of starting from scratch. Dr. Ubelaker makes a practice of protecting himself from any extraneous information or assumptions that the police may have about a case. Sometimes he isn't always successful.

One day a package from an FBI agent arrived on Ubelaker's desk. It contained a bone that had been found at a campsite in Anchorage, Alaska. The bone itself had been badly broken and chewed on by several wild animals, and it would have been chewed to bits had it not been for the metal prosthesis embedded in it. The metal plate was the kind used to correct pseudoarthrosis, a condition in the elderly in which a broken bone is too weak to mend itself. The metal plate is attached to the bone to give it support.

No orthopedic surgeon in Alaska could identify the workmanship, so it was sent to Ubelaker. Because of the metal plate, Ubelaker, like the FBI agents and the Alaskan doctors, assumed that the bone was human. It wasn't until he took a small sample of the bone and looked at it under the microscope that he saw the telltale animal pattern of osteons all stacked up like bricks. Although the prosthesis was of the same make as those used in people, it had been implanted by a veterinarian in a large dog.

There are a number of animal bones that are routinely mistaken for human remains, such as the foot bones of a polydactylous pig (a pig with five toes), the rib cage of a sheep, and the cranium of a hydrocephalic calf (a calf with an enlarged skull due to fluid on the brain). In the right or perhaps wrong context, even the fin of a small whale can be mistaken for a human hand.

Once a case comes to the attention of the police, it has to be thoroughly checked out no matter how bizarre, and it is not enough to say that a bone is not human. The forensic anthropologist has to name the species it does belong to. Eighty-five to ninety percent of the time the species does turn out to be human, and then the real search begins. Who was this person, and how did he or she die?

4

THE SCENE OF THE CRIME

The bones were loosely scattered in a thick stand of oak, maple, and beech trees, and three children who had been out playing near their Pennsylvania home on that September afternoon in 1989, did not know what they were looking at until they saw the chalky white globe of a human skull. Without touching a thing, they ran home to get help. Their parents did not believe that the children had found a body, but the next morning they went to see for themselves and quickly called the police.

Before the police arrived, they had a suspicion of who the person might turn out to be. Back at the station there was a report of a missing woman from New York State, but before they could confirm it they had to collect the remains. The skeleton was incomplete, most of it was lying in a creek bed, but water, soil erosion, and rodents had spread the bones over a wide area. As many of the bones as possible had to be found in order to make a positive identification. They also needed other evidence that might have

Yellow plastic ribbon marked off the 20-foot excavation grids. Markers within the sections indicate where evidence was found. (Kathleen O. Arries)

belonged to the victim or the murderer and could help piece together what happened.

The skull the children had found was taken back to the medical examiners office to be examined and compared with dental records of the missing woman from New York. The dentition (arrangement of the teeth) matched. The woman in the woods was from New York and had disappeared while on lunch break from the printing company where she worked. She had been missing for 16 months.

Kathleen Arries was called in to assist in the recovery of all the bones and evidence. Forensic anthropologists are used to arriving at their office and finding a box of bones collected from a crime scene earlier in the week, but more often forensic anthropologists are being called to the scene of a crime for two reasons. The first is that anthropologists are trained in *archaeological excavation* techniques, which are designed to get the most information from the ground with as little disturbance as possible. A forensic site is treated just like an ancient archaeological site—it is methodically mapped, photographed, and every artifact is cataloged so that police officers can reconstruct the events that led up to a death.

The second reason is that police have come to understand that a forensic anthropologist can learn more from the bones in their original position than from bones collected and put in a box for later examination. The position of the bones can point to murder or accidental death and can reveal the sequence of events.

When Arries arrived at the edge of the woods, she stooped under the plastic yellow ribbon that warned POLICE LINE—STAY OUT. The yellow marker ran from the road into the woods, all the way to the ravine and up the opposite slope. The area to be excavated was marked off in 20-foot sections by string and wooden markers. Makeshift tables of plywood on wooden sawhorses were set up next to sifting screens, which are large square frames with window screening on the bottom used to filter through dirt. Workers from the local police agencies took turns searching through the underbrush looking for artifacts, anything human-made such as a weapon, clothing, cigarette butts, or a footprint. Each item had to be marked with a wooden stake, photographed, and recorded on a map. Other workers emptied shovels full of earth onto the sifters, looking for smaller fragments of bone, teeth, or buttons that otherwise would have been overlooked.

Even the smallest bone could be a clue to a murder. The small bones of the hands can reveal tiny cuts the victim received trying to ward off the slashes of a killer's knife by holding up the palms of their hands. The tiny wing-shaped bone deep in the throat, called the hyoid is the only skeletal evidence of a strangulation. It is crushed when a person is strangled.

For eight days, Arries and the recovery crew worked at the wooded site invisible from the main road and only accessible by two

Police work at makeshift tables and screens to sift through loose dirt, looking for small bits of bone.
(Kathleen O. Arries)

dirt roads leading to a narrow grassy lane. The remains were scattered over an area measuring 200 feet by 300 feet of woods and creek bed.

After every piece of bone was recovered, the police started their reconstruction of the crime. It began on the path near the road where a cigarette butt was found. The killer had probably been smoking and dropped it when he got out of his vehicle. At the edge of the grassy lane, they found a .22 caliber shell casing, suggesting that the killer shot the victim then carried her or forced her to walk into the woods. Deeper into the stand of trees an earring was recovered. Maybe the victim had struggled to get free. Down the sloping ridge were the remnants of her pantyhose, and the other earring, and closer to the creek was her jacket.

In the creek bed, where her body had been dumped, were the bones and the rest of her clothing. After her body had decomposed, the bones were spread by the running water more than 200 feet downstream. The small lighter-weight bones had traveled the farthest from the original site. Some bones such as the femur, fibula, and tibia, and tiny foot bones were found on the opposite side of the path, carried there by rodents and other animals.

With the police detective's reconstructed crime scene, and with help from an informant, a suspect was arrested. The story the informant told the police about the events of that day matched with the trail of artifacts and the story they had to tell. But all the evidence collected in the woods was still not enough for the case to go to trial. The suspected murderer was released, let go on a technicality.

Buried Bones

Most of the bodies found in the woods are discovered by hunters and hikers, but not all bodies are found lying on the surface. Many are buried and would never be detected without the help of an informant to lead the police to the site. Sometimes the burial is accidentally uncovered by road construction, housing developments, or flooding water that erodes the dirt away, revealing the secret underneath. Even with an informant's help, the police may not know what to look for when trying to find a buried body.

The Washington, D.C. police department received a phone call about the body of a woman who had been missing for eight months. The informant said the body could be found buried in a stand of overgrown bushes behind a high-rise apartment complex. The police, sure of the tip, called Douglas Owsley, a physical anthropologist at the Smithsonian. When Owsley surveyed the area, with the police, he could tell immediately that the body was not there because the dirt in the area had not been disturbed.

The earth is made up of layers, and when it is dug up the layers are jumbled mixing the darker soil from the bottom with the lighter colored topsoil. The once compact dirt is loosened and will not be as compact as the soil around it.

A murderer, in a hurry to cover up his or her crime, usually digs the smallest hole possible, just deep enough to hide the body, and level with the ground so it does not attract attention. But over time the earth settles and sinks as the body underneath decomposes. A depression is formed. Frequently a second smaller depression forms in the middle of the larger one when the body cavity full of gases deflates and sinks.

The surface of the soil cracks and separates at a burial site. The plants that once grew there are disturbed and die, or their growth is stunted. Weeds take their place. After many years someone with an experienced eye can spot a burial because of the differences in the earth and foliage, which is why Owsley knew the thicket was untouched.

More information from the informant led the police to the furnace room of the apartment building. There was a long retaining wall with sand behind it. Owsley crawled behind the wall and found the body. "I noticed a depression and a subtle mound in the sand. That's where she was." Had it not been for Owsley's experience the police would have wasted valuable time digging in the thicket behind the building.

A police officer kneels at the edge of a shallow grave where the dirt has been removed to reveal the remains of a woman. The polyester clothes are still intact after nine years in the ground. (Kathleen O. Arries)

The techniques used to recover a buried body are different from those used to recover one on the surface. A team will dig down and around a buried corpse until the surrounding area is lower than the body, which now lies on a platform of dirt. This gives the scientists easy access to the body, enabling them to kneel or walk around it while inside the grave. If possible, the body is lifted out as a whole and placed on a gurney for transport back to the morgue. If the skeleton is very old the bones are taken out one by one and packed in boxes.

Natural Disasters

There are many types of forensic situations, including plane crashes and natural disasters such as earthquakes and hurricanes, that require scientists to set up a temporary morgue in school gymnasiums, military barracks, or municipal garages and identify remains that come in from the volunteer recovery crews. During the 1993 and 1994 floods in the Midwest, forensic anthropologists were asked to help identify the bodies inside caskets that floated up to the surface and were carried away by floodwaters. The caskets were corralled and tied to boats that towed them to dry land. In a cemetery the only means of identification is the headstone that stands firmly in the ground. The coffins and the bodies inside them are not marked with a name or even a plot number, so when they float to the surface they are indistinguishable.

In a situation such as a plane crash or fire, the first consideration is finding out how many individuals are represented by the scattered and fragmented skeletal material. Bones in close proximity of each other are usually from the same person, but frequently bone fragments are spread a great distance and jumbled. Counting the skulls gives an accurate indication of how many people there are, and other individual bones are counted and grouped together. Three femurs, for example, indicate the presence of at least two people, and possibly three, if two of the femurs do not correspond. Bones from the same body will correspond in size, age, and musculature.

The Forensic Response Team

The University of Tennessee has the only forensic anthropological response team in the country that is on call 24 hours a day, seven days a week, ready for any forensic emergency. The response team is led by William M. Bass, Ph.D., and is made up of four forensic anthropology graduate students, two to put on gloves and handle the remains, one to take photographs, and one to record the procedures. They meet police at any site where an unidentified body has been or might be found, arriving in a truck fully equipped with a police radio, shovels, rakes, surgical tools, boots, gloves, and body bags.

Most of the cases that they respond to involve decomposed unidentifiable bodies discovered along the highway by road crews or in the woods by hunters. The key word here is unidentifiable. If the body still has fingerprints or can be visually identified by relatives, then the medical examiner is called in. The medical examiner's expertise focuses on diseases and injuries of the flesh and organs, while the forensic anthropologist's expertise is in disease and injuries of the bone. So the rule of thumb is if a body's organs are decomposed and the skin is sloughing off, the forensic anthropologist gets the call. Bodies that are still in the decomposition stage are up for grabs, but no one fights over them because they smell. Michael Finnegan, from Kansas State University, knows that if a dead body is out in the woods and can be smelled before it is seen, he will probably be called on the case. But there are always unusual cases that don't follow the rules, such as the 1983 explosion of an illegal fireworks warehouse in rural Tennessee.

The explosion was of such force that it could be felt 15 miles away. The top priority for Dr. Bass and the response team that was called to the site was to collect and piece together body parts. For two grueling days they gathered body parts from the surrounding fields, loading them into two refrigerator trucks, one for bodies, and one for parts. Dr. Bass recalled that, "We had a pile of shaved legs and a pile of unshaved legs." The team assumed that the shaved legs probably belonged to females and the hairy legs males. When it came time to piece together the bodies, female legs were matched with female torsos, and male legs with male torsos. The team of graduate students learned that the limbs were very important because an identifying ring or bracelet would be recognized by a relative and clinch the identification.

No matter what a case may be about, the role of forensic anthropologists is clear; they are to examine the bones and report on all the findings. After the preliminary in-the-field analysis, the body is taken to the lab where tissue samples (if there are any) are taken and frozen for later lab tests. Depending on the outcome of the forensic exam the tissue samples can be tested for traces of poison and blood analysis. After that, the forensic anthropologist is free to clean the bones by soaking them in a bath of chemicals and hot water, a process that may take as long as three days for the flesh to be free from an entire body. Whatever the forensic anthropologist learns from the examination is sent to the medical examiner, who is the only one who legally can pronounce the cause and manner of death and sign the death certificate.

∇

5

THE BODY FARM

*B*odies lying out in the open, sunk into a murky pond, and buried in shallow graves in the woods behind a university hospital recall a scene right out of a fictional horror movie, but this scene is real. It is called TARF, the *Tennessee Anthropological Research Facility,* or as some of the founder's colleagues call it, the Bass Anthropological Research Facility, BARF.

William M. Bass first started working at the University of Tennessee in the anthropology department in 1971, and he quickly gained a reputation as a bone expert, receiving bodies from police departments all over the country. He needed a place to keep the bodies that he was being asked to examine, because he knew that the bodies were not only forensic cases that needed to be solved but also useful for researching how a body decays. The university granted Bass the use of two acres of land for his work.

Working with dead bodies does not bother him. "It's a puzzle to me," he says, "a challenge to tell who it was, how it got there, and tell what happened to them." According to Dr. Bass, "When a body comes in, it becomes a research tool," a 206-piece puzzle from the 206 bones in the human body.

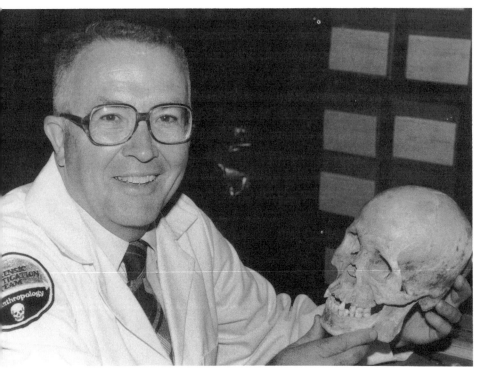

William Bass at the Tennessee Anthropological Research Facility examines one of the skulls processed at the facility. (William M. Bass)

Whenever Bass arrived at a homicide scene, the first question the police would ask him was how long had the body been there. He found that a difficult question to answer because there was very little about how a body decays in forensic literature, so Bass decided to do something about it. He began to record the decay rates of bodies above and below ground. "It may be weird, but how else do you get it done?" he explains, "you can't theorize about it."

To get the bodies, Bass approached the medical examiner and the district attorneys and told them that they were burying a valuable resource when they buried unidentified corpses. Dr. Bass offered to take the bodies for his research, with the promise of returning them for proper burial.

He started by placing bodies on the ground of the 2-acre wooded area, which is surrounded by a chain link fence, topped with barbed wire, and a wooden inner fence to keep out curious students.

Today, the facility "processes" 30 to 40 bodies a year, plus a number of dogs donated by the local animal shelter. "Processing" means letting the decomposition process take its natural course and watching what happens. The bodies in the woods are placed in positions murder victims are most frequently found in and periodically checked by one of the 20 graduate students who record and photograph the advancement of decay. Graduate students record the appearance of the body and its decomposition as well as the change in plant growth, soil conditions, weather, temperature, and the number of insects and their activities. This continues until the body is fully skeletonized.

Dr. Bass and his staff try to be as accurate as possible in their research, recreating many different types of occurrences that are common in forensic work, such as when bodies are wrapped in plastic, buried in shallow graves, lying uncovered on the ground, on concrete slabs, and in the trunks and backseats of cars. Each experiment offers a glimpse of how a body decays in a specific situation.

Some of the research projects are the direct result of current police cases. Dr. Bass worked on an appellate case that involved a man who had been convicted of a double murder 10 years before. When the prosecution reviewed the case file it found contradictory reports. One stated that the victims had been shot in the back, another that they were shot in the front. Dr. Bass found both reports equally confusing and set out to answer a few questions such as what the damage to the sternum (breastbone) looks like when shot from the front verses the back. After examining a human sternum that he had shot in the front, he concluded that the wounds caused to the two murdered men were similar to those he inflicted on the breastbone. Bass's research shed new light on the case and also added new information about a bullet's impact on the sternum.

Another project Dr. Bass's students are working on may answer a question raised by a group of scientists in Australia: How long does it take the ligaments of the front teeth to decay and the front teeth to fall out? Dr. Bass and his students thought it an interesting question and set out to answer it by placing bodies in the ground and digging them up periodically to record the change in the ligaments, until the teeth fell out. They found that it takes between 9 to 16 months for the front teeth to fall out of a skull.

The graduate students have their own research projects. One student is studying the development and decay of *adipocere*. Adipocere, or adipose tissue, is fat that decays in the presence of moisture. The tissue turns a waxy white and decays slowly. There being very little information about how the decay progresses, the student has sunk three bodies in a pond to find out more.

All of this may seem rather unpleasant, but the research is conducted in the most serious manner and the findings have important implications for future forensic work. The difficult task of determining how long a person has been dead has become more precise, and the more precise the forensic scientists are, the more successful the police are in catching killers.

Not only the police rely on Bass's work at TARF. The facility supplies the FBI's DNA lab with hair and bone samples several times a year for research. DNA, or deoxyribonucleic acid, is genetic material. It contains information on all hereditary traits. Living DNA is relatively stable inside cells, but after death some DNA is damaged or lost completely because of enzyme activity. It is unclear how long this process takes. Nobody knows if DNA is altered differently by the decay process in the sun versus the shade, or winter versus summer, but with the help of TARF, the FBI will be able to find out.

Dr. Bass also works with dog trainers who teach dogs to locate buried bodies. These dogs are brought to the facility every three or four months to practice. Ahead of time, Dr. Bass buries bodies at depths of 1, 2, and 3 feet to test the dogs' skill. Experiments with different substances are conducted to see if certain materials such as lime can mask a decaying body's scent and throw the dogs off track.

Rate of Decay

The most important piece of information that Dr. Bass and his students have extracted from all of their research is the pattern of decay. By recording all the subtle changes that occurred on the many bodies processed at TARF, a pattern emerged. After death occurs, the chemicals in the body start to break down. During life, the gastrointestinal tract continuously produces a mucus that protects the living tissue from destruction, but after death the digestive enzymes continue to work without the normal controls of the living body. This process is called *autolysis,* meaning automatic digestion—the body feeds on itself. *Putrefaction,* the major component of decomposition, is a bacterial action. Bacteria are single-celled organisms; some types of bacteria are always present in the body. Bacteria in a living body are like prisoners in a jail, they are kept alive but under control. Once the body dies, the jail bars disappear and the bacteria are freed. They reproduce quickly and feed on the soft tissues of the body, reducing them to a fluid. The bacterial action causes the formation of gases and a rotten egg smell.

Insects, attracted to the body by the smell, come to feed on the flesh and lay eggs, which produce a progression of larvae that also feed on the tissue. Knowing this pattern, scientists can estimate the length of time a person has been dead by the degree to which decomposition has occurred.

The major variable in the pattern is climate. Heat and humidity speed up the process of decay, and cold slows it down. In the heat of a Tennessee August, a body can be completely skeletonized in as little as two weeks. In winter that same process can take months. So the pattern that Dr. Bass has established is not a timetable but a sequence of what happens first, second, third, and so forth. This pattern can be used and modified anywhere in the country. In Vermont, for example, the rate would be slower, and in Florida the rate of decomposition would be speeded up. Extreme climates, however, inhibit decay. The dry heat of the desert causes the water in a body to evaporate so quickly that there is no time for microbes (bacteria and other one-celled parasites) and insects to act on it. The heat dries out skin in the same way that leather is made by tanning. The same process occurs in extremely cold and windy places where bodies are freeze-dried. The wind and below zero temperatures of the Alps preserved the body of a 5,000-year-old man so well that even the delicate tissue of the eyeballs was still intact.

Besides climate, there are other factors that affect the process, such as the type of soil the body is found in. As a rule, bodies on the surface decay faster than buried bodies because insects have easy access, but acidic soils will accelerate the process of decomposition of a buried body. The acid in the soil draws out the calcium phosphate from the bones, making them harder and more brittle. After about 50 years, buried bones appear to be mineralized or petrified, preserving them indefinitely.

Bodies found in the water can be either preserved or completely skeletonized. Sea lice, small crustaceans about a quarter of an inch long, congregate in a cloud of thousands and can clean a body of its flesh in a matter of hours. Divers who recover drowning victims often have to be careful not to let the sea lice onto their skin. In slow moving or standing water, however, fat becomes saturated with moisture and turns into adipocere. Once adipocere forms, it is relatively permanent, preserving bones for years. An almost complete body of a man who died in 1792 and turned to adipocere is on exhibit in the Hall of Physical Anthropology in the National Museum of Natural History, in Washington, D.C.

Sight, Smell, Touch

Once the tissue has decayed and only the bones are left, a lot can still be learned about time since death by what the bones feel like, look like, and smell like. A bone that has a greasy feel to it is called *green bone* and indicates a fairly recent find. Bones stay green above ground for less than a year, but buried bones can retain that greasy feeling for much longer. Bones left lying out on the surface become bleached white and brittle in the sun, losing all their moisture. Bones that have been buried become stained and dark. The color of the bone can indicate whether it has been moved or not. When a bleached white skull is dug from a shallow grave or dark stained long bones are found in a pile above the ground, it's clear that the bones have been moved, intentionally or unintentionally. Exposure to freezing temperatures creates lacy cracking on the surface, indicating that the bones have weathered at least one winter.

Even after all the soft tissue is gone, the long bones will still have a slight odor from the residue of bone marrow inside the bone cavity. It smells like candle wax, and the odor can linger for up to 50 years. Bones older than that are odorless.

The Bug Detective

Insects are the first to arrive at a dead body. Acting like tiny snitches for the police, they provide vital testimony about the time of death. Insect evidence was first used to solve a murder case in 1850, in France. A couple was charged with killing an infant whose body had been dug up from their yard, but the insects found on the dead baby's remains indicated that the child had been dead long before the couple even moved to that house. *Forensic entomology* has been practiced in Europe for more than a hundred years, but in the United States, insects are relatively new members of the forensic team. Their specialty is providing data to determine time of death.

Jeffery Barnes, an entomologist at the New York State Museum in Albany and a forensic consultant for the New York State Police Department, explains that forensic entomology is based on the theory of ecological succession. The insects that come to a corpse arrive in a predictable sequence. The first insects are the glittery greenbottle blowflies. Their scientific name is *Sarcophagi*, meaning corpse eater. The blowfly prefers to lay eggs only in large mammals that have been dead a couple of hours. They begin to arrive within 10 minutes of death, feed on the still warm soft tissue, and lay eggs in openings such as the nose, eyes, mouth, and wounds. The eggs of the blowfly begin to hatch into larvae or maggots within 24 hours. The larvae feed on the soft tissue, preparing it for the next wave of insects, beetles, who prefer dry flesh and bone. After feeding, the larvae will move off the body into the surrounding soil to develop into pupae. Predatory insects such as the rove beetle also come and prey on the insects feeding on the corpse. Each wave of insect invaders is a time marker and can be as accurate as a clock.

Entomologists have known for a long time that insect species follow a very specific pattern in life. This specificity allows the scientists to gauge the insects' arrival at the site and figure out how long a body would have been there. Some insects lay eggs only at high noon, some lay eggs only indoors, or only in the shade, or only in the bright sunlight. Even the absence of insects can be forensic

THE LIFECYCLE OF THE BLOWFLY

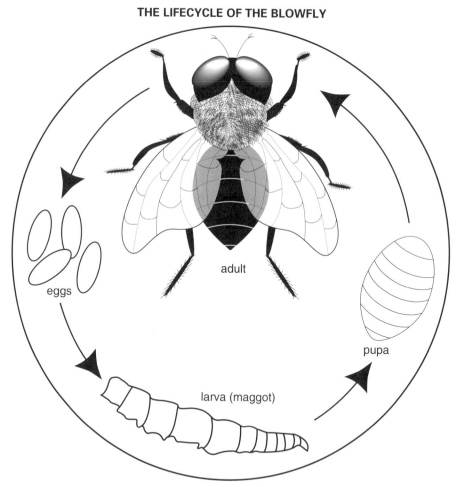

Figure 3 A female blowfly can lay 600 eggs in one day. The larval stage lasts several days to several weeks, after which the larva moves off to burrow into the ground where it transforms to a pupa and then an adult fly.

evidence. If there are no insect larvae on a corpse that is lying outside, the police know that either death just occurred and not enough time has elapsed to attract insects or that death occurred somewhere else and the body has been moved. It might also mean that the body had been frozen. Freezing a body temporarily stops all decomposition, and insects will not be attracted to it until it has thawed.

At a crime scene, samples of the various insects found are collected and put in small vials to be taken back to the lab for analysis. What entomologists are looking for are the most mature specimens, the insects that arrived first and laid their eggs. They hold the key to pinpointing the time of death.

Live immature specimens are brought back to the lab to be raised to adulthood. They are placed in an incubator that simulates the humidity and temperature of the crime scene. If possible, a bit of flesh that the insects had been feeding on should be brought back in order to duplicate the insects' diet. When the eggs hatch, the researcher can count back and determine when the first eggs were laid and how long the corpse had been at that location.

Maggots or larvae, look very much alike from one species to the next. Even to a trained eye it can be difficult to make a positive identification. Rather than identifying the larva, the entomologist raises it and identifies the adult fly.

A case in Hawaii illustrates just how accurate insect time-of-death estimates can be. The body of a 37-year-old man was found by joggers in a swamp on the island of Oahu. The corpse was covered with blowfly larvae. The analysis of the larvae compared with laboratory-reared specimens placed the time of death at 120 hours or five days before the body had been found. Information from the Honolulu police department suggested that the victim had been last seen alive 123 hours before the body was discovered and that the man did not show up at work 121 hours before. The estimate that the insect analysis provided established that it was possible for the murder victim to have been in the company of a man who was subsequently convicted of the murder.

Unfortunately none of the information derived from insects is foolproof. Insect timetables can be delayed or hurried. The big variable is temperature. Along with the insects, entomologists also collect information from meteorologists about the temperature and weather conditions for the area where a body is found. Cool weather slows down insect activity and the growth of eggs and larvae. In winter, eggs laid inside a body will grow slower, and the larvae will stay inside a body longer in order to maintain their own body heat. This situation results in a body that has decayed quickly on the inside but still has intact skin.

Another factor that hinders insect activity is the position of the body. Insects can't get at a body that is wrapped in a rug, sealed in a plastic bag, or buried, which delays the timetable, making insects as time-of-death indicators virtually useless.

The longer the interval between death and discovery of the body, the less accurate the estimate using insect data will be. For forensic anthropologists who see fully decomposed skeletonized bodies, the insects can still be of some use. Accumulated insect casings can give an indication of how many insect life cycles have taken place, and in what season the death occurred.

A skull found in the spring of 1985 in Tennessee had a wasp's nest inside. Wasps will only build their nests in dry places, so the scientists concluded that the skull would have had to have been completely decayed and dry the summer before. It would have taken a year or more for decomposition to be complete and that meant that death occurred in 1983 or earlier. To be sure, the area where the skull was found was searched for more clues and police uncovered a section of vertebra that had a small tree growing through the center of it. The sapling was cut in order to read the tree rings. The tree was also two years old, adding further evidence that the person died at least two years before the body was found.

Bugs on the body are only half of the story. Bugs found on the clothes or even the car of a murder suspect could be the key evidence placing him or her at the scene of the crime. Insects that are specific to a particular area can indicate where a body has been if it has been moved. An urban insect such as a cockroach found on a body lying in a swamp would indicate to the police that death had probably taken place inside someone's home, and the body was then taken to the swamp and dumped.

Underwater Insects

In the summer of 1989, divers exploring the murky waters of the Muskegon River in Michigan discovered a car, and when they peered through its submerged window they saw a female body still buckled into the driver's seat. The police hauled up the car and sent the body to the morgue for an autopsy, which showed that the injuries to the woman's head were not consistent with how the car seemingly plunged into the river. Such inconsistencies usually add up to foul play, and in many cases the police do not have to look beyond the immediate family of the victim for a murder suspect. In this case the victim's husband was suspected of the crime.

The victim's husband claimed that he had last seen his wife in June of 1989. He told police that he and his wife had an argument and she had driven away still angry. It had been a foggy night and perhaps she had lost her way and accidentally plunged into the river. But cocoons found on the car's fender proved him to be a liar. In the winter, black flies are in their larval stage, and in the spring they go underwater in a river or stream and weave cocoons, attaching themselves to rocks or other large hard surfaces such as a submerged car. Because of the cocoons, the forensic entomologist determined that the car had to have been in the water no later than April or May but not as late as June. The husband had killed his wife and dumped her car and body into the river in the spring, long before he reported her missing in June. Insects unmasked another murderer. The husband was convicted and sent to prison.

Forensic entomology is developing at a rapid pace. Entomologists can now determine whether or not a victim was on drugs by testing the insects that fed on the decomposing body. Eventually scientists will be able to test the bug splats on a suspect's car or the sand flies stuck to a suspect's grillwork and use this information to determine who was at the scene of a crime.

6

HIDDEN IDENTITY

*A*ll humans have the same assortment of 206 bones that make up the skeleton, but each person's skeleton is different. Have you ever broken your arm or had a tooth pulled? Do you have flat feet? Are you left-handed? All of these features manifest in the bone and make your skeleton unique.

These skeletal markers are the nuts and bolts of the forensic anthropologists' job in determining sex, race, age, and stature. "Male, negroid, 40 years old and 6 feet 1" is just a police-blotter description that could fit thousands of men, but for detectives it is a first step in identifying a skeleton. More specific information read from broken bones, diseases that affect the bone, deformities, and other trauma from work or sports make the description of the victim even more complete.

Male or Female?

The difference between the male and female skeleton is subtle, and it is difficult to measure with a caliper and ruler. In general, the male skeleton is larger and its bones are more robust (thicker and longer) than the female skeleton's.

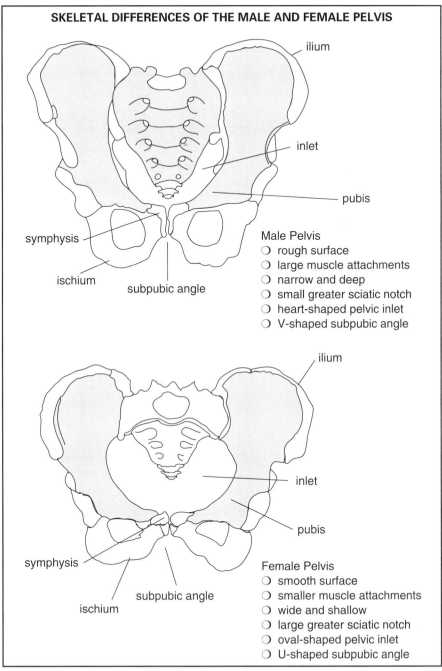

SKELETAL DIFFERENCES OF THE MALE AND FEMALE PELVIS

ilium

inlet

pubis

symphysis

ischium

subpubic angle

Male Pelvis
- rough surface
- large muscle attachments
- narrow and deep
- small greater sciatic notch
- heart-shaped pelvic inlet
- V-shaped subpubic angle

ilium

inlet

pubis

symphysis

ischium

subpubic angle

Female Pelvis
- smooth surface
- smaller muscle attachments
- wide and shallow
- large greater sciatic notch
- oval-shaped pelvic inlet
- U-shaped subpubic angle

Figure 4 The male and female pelvises are different from each other. In general the female pelvis is wide and shallow, and the male pelvis is narrow and deep.

Muscles are attached to the bones, and at the site where they are connected a ridge is formed. The bone becomes raised and rough. The larger the muscle, the larger the ridge. Men usually have larger muscles, so men's bones usually have larger bony ridges.

In the female skeleton, bones tend to be smaller and smoother with fewer bony growths. These general characteristics become less distinct because large, robust women and small men share many of the same characteristics, making it difficult to identify the sex of a skeleton by bone size alone.

The only functional difference between the male and female skeleton is the design of the pelvis. The female pelvis is designed for childbirth while the male pelvis is not. If the pelvis is present at a forensic scene, a forensic anthropologist will be able to tell the sex of the victim with 90 to 95 percent accuracy.

There are three separate bones that fuse during puberty to form the pelvis; the ilium, ischium, and pubis. In general, the male pelvis is narrow and deep, and the opening in the center formed by the two pelvic halves, called the pelvic inlet, is heart-shaped. The female pelvis is wide and shallow, and the pelvic inlet is oval to make it easier for a baby to pass through during childbirth.

On the lower edge of the ilium, the large fan-shaped bone you feel at your hip, there is a notch called the greater sciatic notch. The angle of the notch is narrow in males, less than 50 degrees. In females the angle of the notch is wider, greater than 50 degrees. During a quick check in the field, a forensic anthropologist can measure the notch with his or her thumb. Place the thumb in the notch: if there is room to wiggle it, it is female, if it is a tight fit, it is male.

At the front of the pelvis, six or seven inches below the belly button, the two halves called inominates meet and form the pubic symphysis. Between them, there is a small piece of cartilage that cushions the two bones. During pregnancy a hormone is released that softens the cartilage between the pubic symphysis so that the two bones actually separate during delivery. After delivery the cartilage hardens again. Each softening, separation, and hardening causes pits called scars of parturition to form on the bone. By

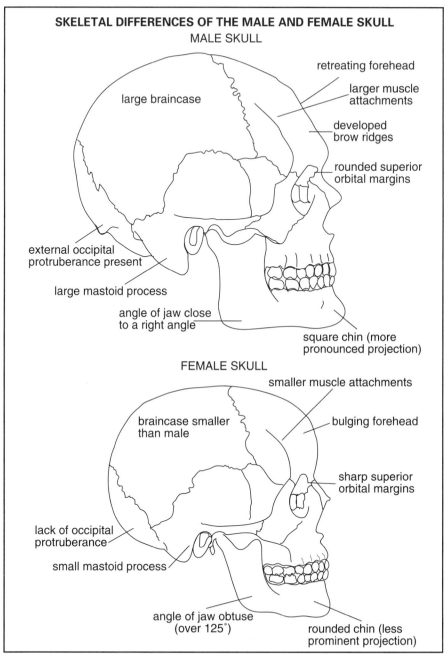

SKELETAL DIFFERENCES OF THE MALE AND FEMALE SKULL

MALE SKULL

retreating forehead

larger muscle attachments

large braincase

developed brow ridges

rounded superior orbital margins

external occipital protruberance present

large mastoid process

angle of jaw close to a right angle

square chin (more pronounced projection)

FEMALE SKULL

smaller muscle attachments

braincase smaller than male

bulging forehead

sharp superior orbital margins

lack of occipital protruberance

small mastoid process

angle of jaw obtuse (over 125°)

rounded chin (less prominent projection)

Figure 5 Skulls of men and women differ. In general, the skull of a male is larger, has more pronounced muscle markings, a heavier jaw, and large brow ridge. The skull of a female is smaller, with fewer muscle markings and rounded or pointed chin.

reading the extent of the scarring on the symphysis an anthropologist can tell if a woman had given birth or not.

The skull is the second most useful set of bones in the human body when it comes to determining the sex of a skeleton. During puberty, as the rest of the body is changing, the skull begins to show signs of male and femaleness. While boys' voices are changing and their faces are sprouting hair, their facial bones become longer, and more prominent. In general, males tend to have a heavier brow ridge over the eyes, and the orbits (eye sockets) are smaller and square with rounded edges. They have a large bump on the lower back of the head, which is a muscle attachment line called the occipital protuberance, and they develop a "Dick Tracy" square chin with heavy mandible (jaw bone). The female skull tends to keep its graceful form—a smaller head, a rounded chin, and fewer muscle markings.

When the pelvis and skull are not present, other bones such as the humerus, ulna, radius (arm bones), scapula (shoulder blade), femur, tibia (leg bones), and even the patella (knee cap) can be used to determine sex, but not as accurately. Even something as inoccuous as the clavicle (collarbone) can be used to determine a skeleton's sex. Most men have broader shoulders than women. Women can have well developed legs, well developed arms and back, but for the most part they do not have shoulders as broad as a man's because of the clavicle. The clavicle acts as a strut pushing the shoulder out to the side. If we did not have a clavicle our arms would swing into our chests similar to the way a cow's front legs are attached to its body. The male clavicle is longer and extends the shoulder out further from the body than women's shorter clavicle.

Because none of the methods of determining sex from a single bone, including the pelvis, are foolproof, most anthropologists agree that more than one bone should be used.

New techniques are always being devised to get better accuracy, but many times the technology is too expensive to be practical. There is a test called the Y-chromosome fluorescence test that detects the presence of the Y-chromosome (the male sex chromosome) in tissue samples that have been stained with quinacrine mustard and viewed under a fluorescence microscope. The test is very accurate and can determine sex of bones that have been dead more than 10 years, but it will be a long time before fluorescence microscopes become standard equipment in police labs because they are so expensive. The skill of an expert is less expensive and can be just as accurate.

Age at Death

Determining how old a person was when he or she died is the second major question in the police-blotter description. The methods depend on finding the universal age indicators that are those parts of the skeleton that change predictably over time in all humans. We all age, but what are the changes that occur to everyone at specific times in our lives? In childhood the changes are noticeable: the skeleton grows taller, bones thicken, teeth appear and fall out and are replaced by adult teeth. But once a person reaches adulthood growth stops and the changes that occur are more due to wear and tear on the body than through the aging process. And wear and tear on the body is different for everyone, depending on the kinds of activities a person does. A 45-year-old marathon runner will have more wear on her legs than a 45-year-old bookworm. Other than age and activity, nutrition, disease, and health all affect the pattern of change in the bone. Because of the deterioration of the bone, a skeleton of a person with osteoporosis appears older than a skeleton of the same age without the disease.

Determining the age of a skeleton is based on how the skeleton is formed. Bones do not grow all in one piece. In many bones, such as the arm and leg bones, the epiphyses form separately from the diaphyses and fuse together in a process called ossification. At birth, a baby has 300 separate bones, and there are 450 centers of ossification that fuse, creating the 206 bones we have as adults. You can actually see how the bones fuse, by holding the bones up to a light, just like holding your hand in front of a flashlight. If there is

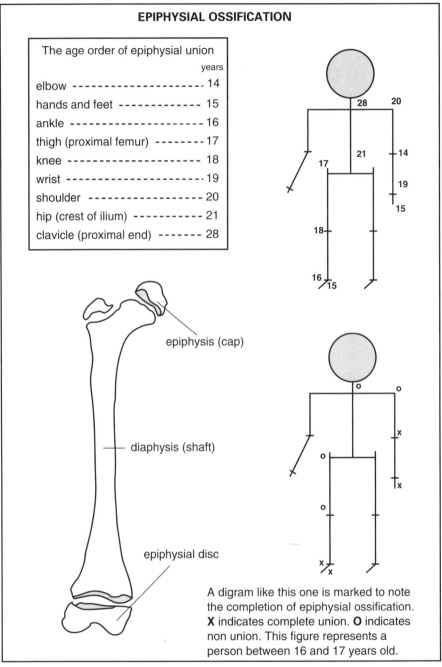

EPIPHYSIAL OSSIFICATION

The age order of epiphysial union

	years
elbow	14
hands and feet	15
ankle	16
thigh (proximal femur)	17
knee	18
wrist	19
shoulder	20
hip (crest of ilium)	21
clavicle (proximal end)	28

epiphysis (cap)

diaphysis (shaft)

epiphysial disc

A digram like this one is marked to note the completion of epiphysial ossification. **X** indicates complete union. **O** indicates non union. This figure represents a person between 16 and 17 years old.

Figure 6 Each bone in the human body completes ossification by a certain age, allowing a forensic anthropologist to determine the age of a skeleton by bone growth.

a slight glow through the bones then they have not fully fused yet. If no light comes through, the bone is solid and completely fused.

Each bone fuses at a different and predictable rate. The two halves of the mandible at the chin's midsection are fully fused by the age of two. The humerus, at the elbow joint, fuses together by the age of 14. The bones of the pelvis complete the growth process by age 21, and the femur near the knee is solid by the age of 18. By 28 the end of the clavicle at the center of the chest is completely fused into one bone.

The skull is also made up of separate bones. An infant's skull bones are thin with space in between to allow the head to be molded and squeezed through the birth canal. After birth, the bones begin to grow and knit together. They fuse slowly, taking an entire lifetime. The squiggly lines on the skull where the bones meet are called *cranial sutures*. The metopic suture that runs down the middle of the forehead fuses by age two. The sagittal suture on the top of the head, running from front to back fuses by age 35. The coronal suture at the front of the skull from temple to temple fuses by age 40. At death these ossification timetables are frozen and if read correctly give accurate age at death.

Once all the bones are fully fused and united, the aging process begins to break bone down. The bones weaken, and joints form bony ridges from long years of use like the rusty buildup on old metal pipes.

The public symphysis that is so instrumental in judging sex is also vital in judging age. As a person ages, the surface of the pubic symphysis becomes more pitted and craggy and can be read like a topographical map and compared with standard markers, which were first mapped out by T. Wingate Todd in 1920 and later revised by Dale Stewart and Thomas McKern in 1957. They looked at hundreds of pubic symphyses and found similarities within age groupings. There was a pattern as to how the bumps and ridges formed as a person got older. Today anthropologists use plaster casts of pubic symphyses at these known stages to compare with unknown symphyses.

There is one problem with this method. The scarring on the female pubic symphysis due to childbirth alters the pattern and is not the same as that found in men. Because the pelvis is subject to childbirth trauma, scientists have been looking for other age indicators. The end of the rib where it attaches to the sternum at the center of the chest shows many of the same changes as the pubic symphysis, without being either a weight-bearing bone or involved in childbirth like the pubic symphysis. The changes that occur on the rib end surface are more uniform in males and females, making them good predictors of age.

To determine the age of a child, an anthropologist looks at the teeth, which are accurate age indicators because they grow and fall out at predictable rates. Baby teeth, or deciduous teeth, start to erupt at seven months and are complete by two years. The permanent incisors and first molars erupt at 6–7 years, lateral incisors at 7–8 years, canines at 10–11 years, first and second premolars

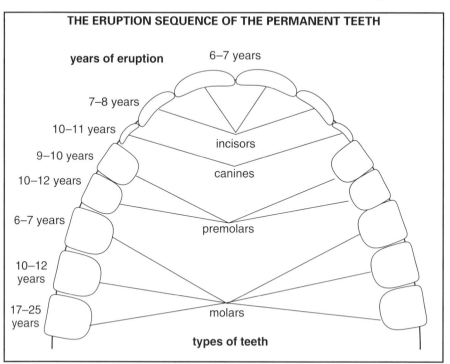

Figure 7 Baby teeth, or deciduous teeth, grow, fall out, and are replaced by permanent teeth at a predictable rate making them useful age indicators.

∇

between 9–12 years, second molars at 10–12 years and third molars between 17–25 years.

In old age when gum tissue is lost, the bone underneath recedes, exposing more and more of the tooth. The phrase "long in the tooth" refers to someone who had lived a long life.

One method that has turned out to be extremely accurate for determining age at death is unfortunately destructive to the bone, and in many cases the anthropologist does not have the permission to damage the bone. While identifying the bodies of dead soldiers for the military, forensic anthropologist Ellis Kerley discovered a new technique for telling the age of a person at death from their internal bone structure. By slicing off a wafer-thin cross section of the femur or other long bone, Kerley could analyze the bone structure under the microscope. A wafer of bone as thin as one-tenth of a millimeter reveals the circular canals or osteons that carry blood and nourishment throughout the bone. Concentric circles form around the osteons resembling the age rings of a tree. The older a person gets, the more fragmented the osteons become, and by comparing the number of healthy osteons to fragmented older ones and applying them to a mathematical equation, the age at death can be calculated. It is an elaborate and time-consuming method, and although it is accurate, it is seldom used in ordinary forensic cases. It might be used in unusual circumstances, and in extraordinary archaeological finds such as the 8,000-year-old skeleton that had been preserved in a cave in Colorado. Using Kerley's method, scientists discovered that the man who crawled into the cave high in the mountains was between 35 and 40 years old when he died.

Race

Race is more of a cultural distinction than a biological one. The only racial variations that exist in the skeleton are found in the shape of the face, particularly the width, length, and forward projection of the bones. But there is a wide range of overlap and mixing of the facial features because of cultural mixing. Still, determining the race of an individual will add to the general description, just as eye color and height.

To determine the race of a skeleton, a forensic anthropologist relies on generalizations. There are three basic skeletal racial groups; caucasoid, negroid, and mongoloid, which includes Asians and Native Americans. The typical mongoloid features include a rounded cranium, flat cheekbones and nasal opening, and shovel-shaped incisor teeth.

The characteristics of the negroid skull include a smooth and elongated cranium with a wide, broad nasal opening. The distance between the orbits is wide, and the alveolar process, the bone between the bottom of the nose and the upper teeth, projects outward.

The caucasoid facial skeleton is rough and elongated. The nasal opening is narrow and long, and the distance between the orbits is narrow. In general, people of European descent have projecting chins. In extreme cases where the jaw extension is pronounced, it is called a Hapsburg jaw after a recessive genetic trait of European royal families resulting from excessive inbreeding. Australian aborigines and some Pacific Islanders, however, have rounded receding chins. People of Hawaiian descent have a distinctive-shaped jaw, called a rocker jaw. When the mandible is placed on the table and gently tapped it will rock like a rocking chair because of the rounded jawbone.

Because the United States is a "melting pot" the distinctions between the races have become blurred, and many times the cultural activities that affect the skeleton indicate race better than biological indicators. In the past some cultures have attempted to manipulate the body structure in an attempt to make it fit the culturally accepted image of beauty. Examples of this are the former Chinese practice of foot binding for upper-class Chinese females and ancient Mayan head molding that resulted in an elongated and flat forehead.

Other cultural deformations were unintentional, such as the ancient Native American practice of using cradleboards to carry

∇

babies. The board molded and flattened the back of the head as the baby was carried for the first years of its life. Today, traditional Puerto Ricans still place tight crocheted caps on their infants to protect them from "bad influences" and may also inadvertently shape the head.

The Pencil Test

The police need to know as much about the victim as possible as soon as possible, and one way to know the race of the victim is using the pencil test. Dr. William Bass discovered that he could tell the race of a skull by balancing a pencil or ballpoint pen on different surfaces of the skull to show alignment and protrusion of the facial bones.

One test attempts to touch one end of a pencil to the chin while touching the other end at the base of the nasal opening. If the pencil lies flat and touches both points at the same time, the skull is usually caucasian. If the pencil does not lie flat because the mouth section is in the way, the skull is probably negroid because of the way the teeth section protrudes.

Another test checks the size of the nasal sill, that little bit of bone at the base of the nose between the two nostrils, by running the pencil gently up into the nasal opening. In caucasoids, the bone will stop the pencil from entering the nose, but in negroids the sill is smaller and the pencil will slide in easily. By laying the skull face up in the palm of the hand, the pencil can be balanced across the nasal opening. If a finger can be slid along the cheekbone underneath the end of the pencil without knocking it off, then the skull is probably caucasoid. This is difficult to do on a mongoloid skull because the face is flatter, rather than pointy like the caucasoid face. Dr. Bass's in-the-field test gives the police a head start in sorting through reports of missing persons who might match the unidentified skeleton.

Measuring a tibia on an osteometric board. (Kathleen O. Arries)

Stature

Estimating the height of a person is a mathematical problem, and height is the physical feature that can most accurately be figured out. In 1875, Thomas Dwight was measuring the heights of skeletons by laying out all of the bones—leg bone by leg bone, vertebrae by vertebrae, leaving tiny gaps for the tissue that fit in between. It was a tedious way to calculate the height of a person, and other scientists were trying to find an easier way. Scientists studied thousands of cadavers to chart the relationship of the individual bones to the total height of a person when they were alive. If the length of the femur was known, for example, could you figure out the total height? Could the same thing be done using the humerus or the tibia?

In 1948, Mildred Trotter along with G. C. Gleser developed a mathematical equation that could do just that. Her work came from the accurate records of World War II and Korean War dead. The only groups not fully represented were women and children, but since then more studies have been conducted and Trotter's calculations have been revised to include these groups. The equations vary slightly for different races also because of the slightly different proportions that exist between the long bones and the total height.

Most forensic anthropologists today still use Trotter and Gleser's method. It is based on a regression analysis, which is a math equation that allows them to determine an unknown measurement such as a person's height from several related measurements such as the length of a leg bone or arm bone. The process is similar to calculating the amount of paint needed to cover a whole room based on the amount of paint used to paint one wall. Fortunately there are regression tables that do the math.

A long bone such as the femur is measured on an *osteometric board*, which looks like a large bookend with one fixed end and one movable panel. The bone is placed on the calibrated board with the lower end of the femur touching the fixed end while the movable panel is adjusted to touch the top of the femur, just like measuring a foot at the shoe store. The measurement is read, and then it is located on the Trotter-Gleser chart under the heading *femur*. In the corresponding column labeled *stature* a number is given in inches. For example, if a femur of a female Caucasian measures 473mm (about 19 inches), on the chart the corresponding number in the stature column is 67. The woman was approximately 67 inches tall or 5 feet, 7 inches.

The height, sex, age, and race of a person gives the police enough information to start looking for a possible identification for the victim. If there is no match, the anthropologist goes back to the bones to search for more details.

7

WE ARE
WHAT WE DO

*A*fter determining the sex, age, race, and stature of the deceased, the next step is to look for any identifying characteristics such as old injuries, diseases, and unusual features such as bowed legs, a prominent chin, or four fingers on the left hand. While forensic anthropologists examine the bones, they also collect information about the deceased such as health records, medical and dental X rays as well as interview relatives about the way the person walked, looked, and if he or she had ever had surgery or a broken bone. The medical data can then be compared to the skeletal data.

If a missing person was known to have had a broken left arm, an old X ray will show a faint line as the scar of the fracture. The left humerus of the skeleton is then x-rayed, and the two X rays are compared. If the skeleton and the missing person are one and the same, the X rays of the arm bones will be exact. If they are not, the scientist can be certain that the skeleton and the missing person are two different people.

Unfortunately many murder victims do not have up-to-date medical records or dental X rays. In cases like these, the bones are still the primary source of information, and the more that can be read from the bones, the more complete the picture of the victim will be. Was the person left handed or right? What diseases bothered him while he was alive? What did she do for a living, and where did she live?

Occupational Trauma

When William Shakespeare wrote *A Midsummer Night's Dream,* he named one of the characters in the play Bottom. Bottom was a weaver, and the name amused 17th-century audiences who knew about the condition called "weaver's bottom." Weavers sat on hard wood floors in front of their looms all day, every day, and over the years bony growths formed on their ischium (backside of the pelvis), because of the chronic inflammation of the surrounding tissues. This painful condition made the bones bumpy and rough.

Other jobs impact the skeleton as well. Over the years research has led to the identification of other physical ailments associated with a particular occupation. Among them: stenographer's spread, similar to weaver's bottom, in which the pelvis gets thicker and wider; florist's fingertips, an arthritic condition that affects the bones in the fingers; and housemaid's knee, the deterioration of the knee joint from constant kneeling and bending. There also is milker's neck, which was common among farmers who milked their cows by hand, with their heads leaning against the cow's side. When the cow shifted its weight it pushed into the farmer's neck jamming, or compressing, the vertebrae in the spine.

In the 1950s when bobby pins were in fashion, girls would get a characteristic chip in the front tooth where they habitually slid a bobby pin into their mouth to open it before securing it in their hair. Similarly, tailors and seamstresses would have a small notch on their front teeth where they held pins in their mouth while working, and habitual pipe smokers develop a worn edge on their front teeth from gripping a pipe tightly. People from many other cultures show similar wear from using their teeth as a tool or a third hand.

In general, if you work one part of your body more than another over a long period of time it will be reflected in the bone. The larger a muscle grows, the larger the bone underneath it has to be to hold the muscle. For example, large ridges on the femur (thigh bone) indicate a well-developed abductor magnus muscle, which is a characteristic of horseback riders who grip the sides of the horse with their thighs. Ridges on the humerus are characteristic of someone who lifts heavy weights such as a body builder, furniture mover, or trash collector.

You can also tell if a person played a musical instrument from his or her bones. Musicians who play woodwind instruments such as the clarinet or oboe use the little cheek muscles to force air through the reeds of the instrument, thrusting the lower jaw forward. Doing this every day for years will produce small bumps on both sides of the mandibular condyles, the knobs that fit into the hollows of the skull forming the hinge of the jaw. Lawrence Angel, formerly of the Smithsonian, was able to determine that the large prominent muscle attachments on the clavicle (collarbone) of a dead man were evidence that he had been either a trumpet or trombone player. Angel mentioned this to the police who then were able to identify the victim as a local musician.

The 1980s brought new skeletal trauma such as breakdancer's knee as well as manhole syndrome suffered by joggers who fell down open manholes. Health club groupies became inflicted with machinery knee. With repeated use even the simplest activity can leave marks on the bone. The things we do today may become imprinted on our bones and years from now we may have "couch potato buttocks," "remote control thumb," or "Nintendo wrist."

Handedness

Being right-handed or left-handed over the years changes the appearance of the bones in the more dominant arm. The ball of the humerus fits into the socket of the scapula (shoulder blade). With regular use the interior of the socket becomes beveled and a slight groove forms. If you are left-handed, your left shoulder socket will have greater beveling than your right arm. The arms of a person who plays baseball for a living or swings a hammer or throws a football will show even greater disparity. The dominant arm will also be slightly longer than the other arm by a few millimeters in order to compensate for the more work it does.

Michael Finnegan, remembers one case he worked on that tested his knowledge of handedness. Remains were brought in by the police, and judging from the skull and pelvis they appeared to be of a female between 30 and 40 years old. Examining the skeleton for other details, Finnegan noticed that the woman had a very well-developed left deltoid process, the outer edge of the shoulder. There was a bony ridge there suggesting that she was left-handed, but the interior surface of the shoulder socket clearly indicated that she was right-handed.

The woman's tibia (lower leg bone) had large ridges where strong calf muscles would have been attached. Finnegan had seen this before in cowboys who wore high-heeled boots and in woman who wore high-heeled shoes a great deal of the time. Sometimes the shortening of the muscle is so pronounced that the person has difficulty walking in bare feet, pushing their heel down flat to the ground.

The discrepancy in the shoulder wear of the female skeleton combined with the wear on the leg bones, got the scientist thinking about what kind of occupations could produce such skeletal markings. Finnegan came up with the idea that the woman had been a waitress who carried large trays high over her head with her left hand and served dishes and drinks with her right hand. He also concluded that the woman probably wore high-heeled shoes as part of her work uniform. When the police identified her remains it turned out that he had been correct—the woman had been a professional waitress.

Disease and Illness

The body of a woman remained hidden in a hastily dug shallow grave until rainwater rushing down the steep ravine exposed the left side of her skull. Just enough was visible to attract the attention of a dairy farmer out for a walk, and he called the police. The body was just 100 yards from where a psychic had taken police nine years before in an unsuccessful search for a missing woman.

When the forensic anthropologist arrived, much of the dirt that had covered the body had been removed, but the dark, soil-stained remains were almost indistinguishable from the surrounding dirt. The skeleton was sheathed in a polyester nightgown and a fuzzy blue-green bathrobe still tied at the waist. The small bones of the feet were still inside dark blue socks, although some scavenging animal had pulled one sock several feet away.

The body was removed and taken back to the police station to be examined. There, the anthropologist determined that the woman had been in her early 20s, about 5 feet 10 inches tall, and Caucasian. The anthropologist also discovered that the woman had a condition called scoliosis, which is curvature of the spine, and had two steel rods surgically implanted into her back. There was only one missing woman that fit that description, and she had been missing for nine years.

Scoliosis and the surgical implants provided the evidence that was needed to establish the woman's identity. X rays taken of the skeleton's spine were compared with medical X rays taken before the woman died. They were an exact match.

The vertebral column of a victim. A cotton swab marks the groove where a steel rod had been surgically implanted in the victim's spine. (Kathleen O. Arries)

Anthropologists look for medical conditions that affect the bone in order to prove or substantiate identification. Most conditions, however, are not as obvious as surgical implants. Many diseases such as arthritis, severe anemia, and osteoporosis affect the bone by stunting growth or leaving scars. By themselves they are good identifying markers, but some diseases offer more information such as race affiliation. Sickle-cell anemia primarily affects people of African descent, and in its severest form it can leave scars on the bone. Thalassemia is another form of anemia that occurs mainly in people of Mediterranean descent.

Some diseases are specific to people who perform certain jobs. Brucellosis, for example is a lung disease that causes lesions to form on the vertebrae. The bacteria that causes it is carried by cows, and the disease affects farmers, meat packers, and people who drink unpasteurized milk.

Kienbock's disease affects the hand bones of carpenters and riveters who spend long periods of time repeatedly pounding with their hands. A similar condition called carpal tunnel syndrome is now being found in people who work long hours on a computer.

Some diseases occur only in certain geographical locations, and if an anthropologist comes across the signs of such a disease in a skeleton he or she can assume that the person had spent some time in that part of the world specific to the disease. For example, mycetoma is a condition that affects the foot. The fungi that cause it thrive in hot and humid locations, and the condition is found in people who have spent a large amount of time in the tropics.

Other kinds of diseases are contracted from the food we eat and water we drink. Excess minerals taken in through impure drinking water are stored in the bone and can leave a person crippled or stunt his or her growth. When small pieces of bone are ground down and put through chemical analysis, they reveal concentrations of the minerals that the body absorbed over a lifetime. Certain geographical areas are known to be rich in certain minerals. For example, India, Taiwan, and parts of Texas have water supplies that contain high levels of fluorine. If a body is found to have suffered from fluorosis, excessive intake of fluorine, then it is safe to assume that the person spent a great deal of time in one of those areas.

Other health problems such as malnutrition and dental neglect show up as eroded tooth enamel, cavities, bowing of the long bones, and signs of growth arrests, indicating that a person probably lived in poverty. A well-nourished person has well-rounded shafts of the long bones and strong teeth. Signs of extensive dental work would indicate that a person had a certain amount of wealth. However, 100 years ago the opposite would have been true. The rich ate cavity causing sugars, whereas, the poor ate mostly grains, fish, and meat and did not suffer from as many cavities.

Positive Identification

After measuring the tibia on the osteometric board, examining minute bumps under the magnifying glass and feeling the depth of knitting between the cranial sutures, a forensic anthropologist has to step back and look at the bones. What do all of the measurements and criteria mean? Was the woman pretty? Was she healthy? Was she in need of a dentist? Did the man limp? Was he in pain? These are the types of descriptions that will help the police identify the missing person.

When all the pieces fit, and the bone analysis matches the information about a missing person, all that is left to do is confirm the positive identification (ID). This is done a number of ways. The first method is to use fingerprints, but this is not always possible. If a body is so badly decomposed that it cannot be identified visually, then chances are the fingerprints are unreadable also. But there are other kinds of prints that can be used, such as sinus cavity prints. On an X ray, a person's sinus cavity shows a scallop-shaped pattern at the top edge. Sinus prints were used in 1978 by a team of forensic scientists appointed by a congressional committee to review the medical data surrounding the assassination of John F. Kennedy. Rumors of a body switching conspiracy had spread, and a forensic team used X rays of Kennedy's sinuses before and after death to conclude that the remains were indeed of Kennedy and not some-one else.

Not everyone has had their sinuses x-rayed, but most people do have their teeth x-rayed at the dentist's office, and like sinuses, teeth are unique identifying features. Scientists who specialize in comparing and matching dental X rays with skeletal X rays are called *forensic odontologists.*

Genetic Fingerprinting

DNA is the building block for every living thing. Everyone has a unique set of DNA that carries the genetic information that determines what every cell in the body will be and how it will function. The DNA analysis, also known as genetic fingerprinting, is a way of unlocking the DNA from the cells so it can be dissolved in enzymes that separate the DNA molecule into thousands of pieces. The genetic material is then sorted by size and exposed to special radioactive probes that focus on specific DNA landmarks. X-ray films of the material look like rows of short and long blurry spots similar to a grocery item's bar code. The radioactive probes are highlighted to show what size piece of DNA the landmark is located on. The pattern is compared with other tests done on other samples of hair, blood, or tissue. The DNA analysis compares only three to six sections of DNA, which is a small fraction of the 3 billion chemical units that make up a person's genetic heritage. If the test compared all the DNA material, there would be no doubt about the match. A match would be 100 percent conclusive. Since the test only compares a small section of DNA, researchers have to look at the frequency with which the exact pattern would occur in a large population. There is about a one in a million chance that another person has the same pattern on those six sections of DNA that you carry in every cell in your body. Some scientists say that frequency is higher, some say it is lower. One in a million is pretty good odds, but the test procedure itself has come under attack. The test is

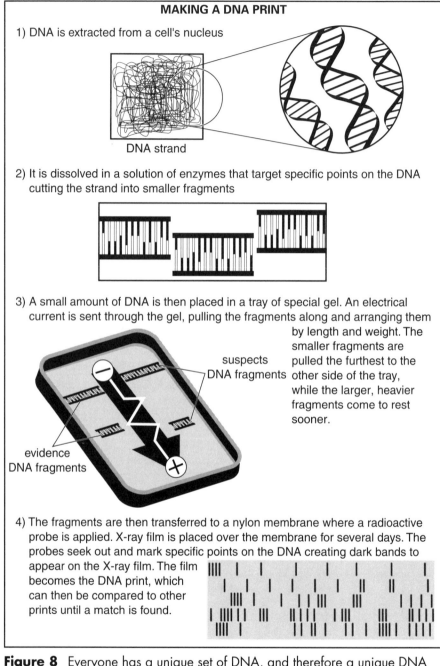

MAKING A DNA PRINT

1) DNA is extracted from a cell's nucleus

DNA strand

2) It is dissolved in a solution of enzymes that target specific points on the DNA cutting the strand into smaller fragments

3) A small amount of DNA is then placed in a tray of special gel. An electrical current is sent through the gel, pulling the fragments along and arranging them by length and weight. The smaller fragments are pulled the furthest to the other side of the tray, while the larger, heavier fragments come to rest sooner.

suspects
DNA fragments

evidence
DNA fragments

4) The fragments are then transferred to a nylon membrane where a radioactive probe is applied. X-ray film is placed over the membrane for several days. The probes seek out and mark specific points on the DNA creating dark bands to appear on the X-ray film. The film becomes the DNA print, which can then be compared to other prints until a match is found.

Figure 8 Everyone has a unique set of DNA, and therefore a unique DNA print. But the print only maps a small percentage of the total DNA, so there is a slight chance—1 in a million—that another person might have the same print.

complex, and the more complicated it is and the more people involved in the procedure, the more chance there is for error.

Until recently, anthropologists have not been able to use DNA prints because it is difficult to find large amounts of intact DNA in old bones once the soft tissue has decayed. A new technique called polymerase chain reaction extracts DNA from seemingly dry bones that still have a trace of collagen or protein left, and magnifies it for study. The scientists who have developed this technique have extracted and copied DNA from a human fossilized femur more than 5,000 years old.

Some scientists worry that DNA fingerprinting will overshadow other identification techniques, but Dr. William Maples of the University of Florida and C.A. Pound Human ID Lab is not concerned about his job security, because as he points out, the goal is to compare the samples of unknown DNA with samples of known DNA. The body has to be tentatively identified by bone analysis before a living relative can be located to donate blood for DNA testing. Bone analysis offers the first clue of identity, which can be readily confirmed or denied if there are available fingerprints or X rays. DNA analysis may be almost foolproof, but it is also expensive and time consuming. A DNA test takes a month to complete, whereas fingerprints, bone analysis, and X-ray comparison are quicker, easier, and less expensive to use and, when used in combination, just as accurate.

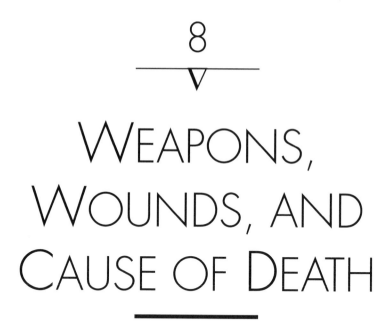

8

WEAPONS, WOUNDS, AND CAUSE OF DEATH

*D*ouglas Owsley of the Smithsonian held up the skull of a murder victim that had two large holes in the cranium. Most people might have thought they were bullet holes, but to Owsley they were unmistakably the result of a hammer. The edges of the holes were depressed, indented as if they had been pushed in, with the pieces still rattling around inside. A bullet is propelled with much more force than a hammer and creates a larger more destructive hole. Anthropologists must be able to determine the difference between a bullet hole, a hammer wound, and a cracked skull. The difference may be that between accidental death and murder, and a matter of plain physics.

When a moving head hits a fixed object with sufficient force, the skull is cracked open. This would happen if someone fell hard to the ground, but when a moving object hits a fixed head, the result is a depressed fracture. This happens if someone is hit with a hammer. The force of the blow, the angle of the blow, and the weapon used in the attack can all be determined from the damage to the bone.

Living bone is primarily made up of calcium, phosphate, collagen, and water. Even though bones may seem to be hard as rock, they are actually pliable and soft, which is why what happens to our bones during our lifetimes remains evident even after death. After death, the bones dry out, becoming harder, stiffer, and brittle. Taking a hammer to living bone and to dead bone will result in different kinds of damage. Living bone is crushed. Dead bones shatter. Because of the different breaking patterns, forensic anthropologists can tell if damage to the bone occurred before death, *perimortem*, or after death, *postmortem*. Perimortem trauma can be split into two categories, that occurring years, weeks, or days before death, and that occurring at the time of death, causing death. Postmortem injuries to bone include chewing on the bones by rodents, splits and cracks to the bone from root growth, and scrapes and cut marks from a killer dismembering the body and trying to get rid of the evidence.

While a person is alive, his or her body has the ability to heal and repair itself. A broken leg, for example, takes up to five months to heal. It heals just as a cut on the skin does. As new bone grows, it knits the two halves together again. The first visible sign that a bone is healing are the shiny rounded edges at the break site. When it is completely healed the break in the bone will have a scar just like a deep cut on the skin forms a scar. On an X ray, the scar will appear as a fine line and will remain visible by X ray for thousands of years. When a person dies, his or her ability to heal dies also. A bone that is broken at the time of death will not heal. The edges will not become shiny or rounded, but will remain jagged and sharp.

Old Murders

Seven percent of Americans who die in this country every year are intentionally murdered or are victims of accidents or suicide. Every one of these deaths will be investigated, but one-third of the murders will not be solved, and many murders mistakenly labeled natural deaths will go undetected. To solve more homicides, they have to be detected first. Many of the homicide cases that never come to trial are cases that involve skeletal remains. Trauma at the skeletal level can be tough to decipher, but not impossible. "All skeletal interpretation can be difficult," Douglas Ubelaker notes. "A lot of these cases take us to the edge of our knowledge. My approach has always been that we have to be creative and responsive to the problems that are presented to us, and sometimes if we don't have the knowledge immediately we can find the knowledge in the collection (33,000 skeletons at the Smithsonian Institution) or through experimentation."

Chicken Legs and Finger Bones

One such case Ubelaker worked on involved a Puerto Rican girl who had been found murdered and left in a Virginia berry patch. Ubelaker's predecessor at the Smithsonian, Larry Angel, had worked on the case and noted that one of the girl's fingers had been cut off. The police had no other leads and the girl's body was returned to Puerto Rico for burial. As if knowing that it would be needed someday, Angel packed the bones and placed the finger bone in a small plastic bag and labeled it.

Years later, new evidence was uncovered by police. Larry Angel had died, so Ubelaker made the trip to Puerto Rico to *exhume* the body. In the small coffin he found Angel's note along with the finger bone in the plastic bag. Angel had not known what caused the trauma, and now it was up to Ubelaker to find out.

The bone had a straight almost clean cut at one end. It did not have the parallel cut marks of a knife, and it did not have the gnawing marks of a rodent, but nothing could be ruled out just yet. What had caused the finger to be cleanly cut like that?

Inspired by the supermarket display of chicken legs that he was buying for a Memorial Day picnic, Ubelaker decided to experiment.

Chicken bones are different from human bones. Animal bones are denser, but the leg of a chicken and the finger of a human are close in size and thickness and in a purely experimental setting may give some clues as to the type of trauma that occurred.

With the raw skin and meat still on the bone, Ubelaker sliced one chicken leg with a sharp kitchen knife, and another with a dull kitchen knife. He chopped another in half with a machete, and another with a mattock, a large flat pick ax. Three more bones, held in place and not held in place, were slammed in a car door. The last chicken leg was run over with the lawn mower, which is a common occurrence for bodies that have been dumped along the roadside in tall grass.

Each chicken leg was labeled and set in boiling water to cook all of the meat away. After the bones were cleaned, Ubelaker examined the kinds of trauma that resulted. The knife cuts showed the shape of the edge of the knife blade, and the bone run over with the mower was completely destroyed. The trauma left by the mattock and the car door seemed similar to that of the girl's finger bone, but since there was no other trauma on the skeleton that would suggest that the killer bludgeoned the victim, it seemed to make sense that at the time of death, the girl's finger had been cut off in the killer's car door.

Ubelaker's experiment did not provide enough evidence for the prosecution. The attorneys needed to know if the experiment would work with a 1974 Pinto, which was the make and model of the car driven by the suspect. Ubelaker and the police located a citizen willing to have a chicken leg slammed in the door of his 1974 Pinto and they conducted another 18 experiments. Only one experiment produced the clean sheared-off cut similar to the one on the victim's finger. It seemed quite possible that the finger had been cut off in a car door. The suspect, with all the evidence mounting against him, confessed.

Although this case never was brought to trial, and Ubelaker's findings were never presented, the extensive work that Ubelaker did will help to increase the knowledge base for all forensic scientists.

Rodents' Chew Markings

Peter Andrews, the curator of paleoanthropology at the Natural History Museum in London, England, lives in a rural area of Wales where he conducts his research on scavenging patterns of animals. He leaves animal carcasses on the hillside near his home and observes what happens to them. Mice, fox, dogs, and even deer will pick up old bones and carry them off, scattering a skeleton over a great distance. Andrews records which animals are most likely to take which bones and how their chew marks vary.

Rodents such as mice and rats have a pair of front teeth shaped like little chisels, and they leave parallel gouges on the long bones of animals. They prefer to gnaw on the long bones in the same way most people eat corn on the cob, nibbling along sideways. If you were to bite into a thick bar of chocolate, the tooth marks left in the chocolate would be similar to the ones rodents leave on bone.

Foxes leave very different shaped marks on bone. They prefer to chew on the knobby ends of the long bones the way dogs eat a soup bone, propping the bone up between its paws, chewing off the ends, and boring small cone-shaped holes into the edges of the bone with their tiny sharp canine teeth. Deer and sheep break the bones by stepping on them in order to get to the nutritious marrow in the center.

In a forensic situation an anthropologist would be able to determine whether an animal gnawed on the bones after death occurred or if a killer mutilated the body at the time of death, which is an important distinction to make. Similar trauma markings found at different homicide scenes may link the crimes and point to the possibility of a serial killing spree.

Weapons

Forensic scientists make it their business to know what kinds of weapons leave what kinds of marks on bone. When police presented Michael Finnegan with a skull that appeared to have a bullet hole, they wanted to know what caliber bullet made that hole. Michael

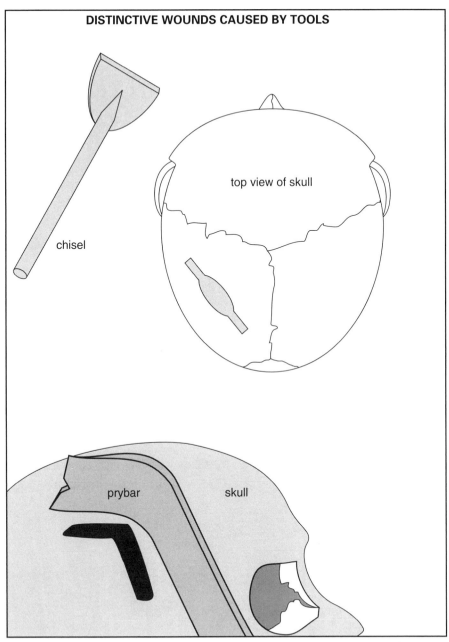

DISTINCTIVE WOUNDS CAUSED BY TOOLS

chisel

top view of skull

prybar

skull

Figure 9 Tools used as weapons leave distinctive wounds. *At top*: The perforation in the left side of the skull was caused by the rarious cross sections of the chisel as it passed through the bone. *At bottom*: The shape of this injury corresponds precisely with the angle and shape of a pry bar similar to the one used by the murderer.

Finnegan measured the hole and suggested that it might have been a .25. That caliber bullet would be rather rare these days, and an officer asked if Finnegan meant a .22 caliber bullet, which would seem more likely. No, said Finnegan, it was definitely a .25, and he could also name the model of the weapon—a Black & Decker. Thoroughly confused, the officer questioned Finnegan again.

"You mean a Smith and Wesson?"

"No," Finnegan held firm. "A Black & Decker. It's a drill hole." As it turned out, the old skull had been a morbid tavern decoration and had been drilled a long time ago to add to its mystery.

Other weapons or tools used as weapons leave signature marks. Circular saws leave curved lines. Saber saws leave regular, straight cuts, handsaws leave straight but uneven marks, and serrated knives leave a scalloped-edged cut. Dull objects produce a U-shaped depression whereas a sharp knife makes a V-shaped notch. Tools, such as a tire iron, leave imprints in the skull that are so distinctive that afterward the tool can be fitted into the traumatized area. Experts at the FBI and forensic specialists around the country learn to recognize the effects of different weapons through experimentation. Cow bones from a butcher shop come in handy to practice on and can be used to compare different kinds of damage from different implements.

When a knife is plunged into a body, it is almost certain that it will hit some bone on the way in. The ribs are a good place to look

A cut mark made
by a knife.
(Kathleen O. Arries)

for fatal blows that have reached the heart and lungs. As the knife pushes its way through bone, it moves the bony material along with it, leaving the back edge of the cut splintery, just as a saw through wood leaves the back edge rough and jagged. This can be felt with the fingertips, and it indicates if a person was stabbed in the front or the back.

Wounds found on the bones of the palm and forearms indicate that the victim may have defended his- or herself by holding up the arms to protect the face and body. The angle of those slashes is also a clue as to whether the killer is right- or left-handed. The sequence of stab wounds or gunshot wounds can also be determined by examining their depth and position.

Burned Bones

In 1993, a religious cult called the Branch Davidians holed up inside the walls of its Texas compound after federal law officers demanded the surrender of the group's firearms. The leader of the group, David Koresh, held the marshals at bay for nearly two months, before federal troops broke down the compound's walls with tanks, and threw in tear gas in hopes that Koresh and his followers would run out. But that did not happen, instead, the buildings burst into flames and burned to the ground. When the fires subsided 86 people had died. Rumors spread that the religious leaders had killed some of their followers, and there had been a mass suicide. Other rumors said that the troops had murdered the people by starting the fire. What really happened? Only the bones will tell.

The bones pulled out of the smoldering cinders were sent to Dr. Ubelaker at the Smithsonian. He and other scientists are looking for signs of trauma such as bullet wounds, and they will determine whether a body was dead before or after it was burned. No matter how many people the FBI interview, the answers will come down to the bones of the only people who were there, and the expert eyes of forensic anthropologists.

Many murderers try to cover up their crimes with fire, but what they do not know is that a body does not burn up completely. To do that would require a fire well above 2,500 degrees Fahrenheit to burn for more than 18 hours. A typical house fire ranges from 900 to 1,800 degrees and lasts no more than six to eight hours. Although burned remains may be charred and shattered, they still hold a wealth of information. Experts can tell that a person was unconscious or dead during a fire when the body is found lying face up, rather than face down as if someone succumbed to the heat and smoke.

The Case of the Body in the Burned Out Car

On Christmas Day, 1988, deer hunters found the remains of a burned-out car, but it wasn't until the next day after a second closer look, that they saw burned bone fragments, teeth, and a Seiko watch where the front seat once was. The sheriff's department called in Dr. Edward Waldrip, the director of the Southern Institute of Forensic Science, to look at the remains. From the damage to the bones and the car, Waldrip estimated that the fire had burned as hot as 2,000 degrees Fahrenheit for at least two hours.

The few fragments sifted from the charred rubble told Waldrip that the victim had been a man with a small build. There was so little left of the man that Waldrip was forced to use an arm bone to calculate height. An arm bone is not a very accurate indicator of height, but it told Waldrip that the man was between 5 feet 4 inches to 5 feet 10 inches tall. The man was 25 to 30 years old, give or take five years. He was also disabled. "He had a marked smaller left leg," Waldrip said. "The bones of the knee were also smaller on the left." The man would have walked with a limp.

There were no other signs of trauma on the skull, rib, or chest fragments to indicate anything other than suicide, but there was so little left of the body that homicide could not be ruled out just yet.

While Waldrip examined the bones, the sheriff's department tried to find the owner of the burned-out car. They knew it was a Fiat, but all other identifying numbers and license plates had been removed. The Fiat company in Italy informed the police of a secret registration number that the owner may not have been aware of. The number was still on the car and led the police to a Fiat dealership in California, and then to the original owner who claimed she had sold the car to a Vietnamese man.

Once the sheriff had the name of the owner, the rest of the pieces fell into place. Relatives described the man as small, about 5 feet 6 inches tall and weighing only 100 pounds. He was 32 years old and suffered from muscular dystrophy, a disease that causes the muscles to gradually deteriorate. In fact the last time he was seen,

Edward Waldrip sits at a table full of burned bone fragments. He pieces them back together like a skeletal jigsaw puzzle. (Kathleen O. Arries)

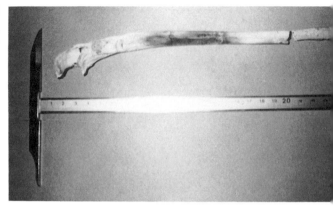

A tibia reconstructed from burned fragments. (Kathleen O. Arries)

at Thanksgiving, the man had mentioned being so disabled that he was contemplating suicide. Members of his family remembered also that he wore a Seiko watch.

A check on the man uncovered that he had been arrested in 1986 near Billings, Montana, for having no identification on the car and for having 50 pipe bombs, gasoline, charcoal briquettes, and gunpowder in the car. He told police that he intended to commit suicide and leave no evidence behind because he did not want to live with the advanced stages of muscular dystrophy. It seems that two years later he was still intent on his plan, but this time no one was there to stop him.

9

FACE FINDING

*T*here is a saying that beauty is only skin deep. That may be true, but the design of the face goes to the bone. Whether you have a jutting chin, big cheeks, a narrow nose, large eyes, or a big smile is all determined by the contours of the skull.

The first person to realize this was a German anatomist, Wilhelm His. In 1895, he studied the heads of 24 male and four female cadavers. It seems gruesome, but his research required him to stick pins into various points on the face until he struck the bone. Marking the pin and pulling it out again he could measure the thickness of the tissue, skin, fat, and muscle that make up the face.

Dr. His discovered that the thickness of the tissue varied on different parts of the face; the skin that cushions the cheek is thicker than that stretching over the forehead but thinner than the tissue padding the chin. You can find that out by feeling your own face, but Dr. His's real discovery was that the thicknesses of flesh on each part of the face remained fairly constant from person to person. For instance, Caucasian men's faces measure up like this: the depth of tissue at the thickest spot, which is just below the nose and above the upper lip, is $11^1/2$ millimeters. The thinnest spot, which is one-third of the way down the nose where the nasal bone ends and the cartilage begins, is only 2 millimeters deep.

If all of our skin measures up the same, then why do we all look so different? The determining factor is not the flesh, but the bone underneath.

Dr. His believed he could apply clay to an actual skull and construct a recognizable face. The skull he wished to reconstruct was believed to be that of Johann Sebastian Bach, the great 18th-century composer who had been dead and decomposing for more than 100 years by the time Dr. His finished the facial reconstruction. Dr. His relied on a sculptor to translate the skull tissue measurements onto the actual skull, and the end result was a bust that looked surprisingly similar to Bach.

Reconstruction

Reconstructing a famous person's face attracts a great deal of public interest and helps researchers prove how accurate reconstruction can be, but is it possible to reconstruct a face from a skull of an

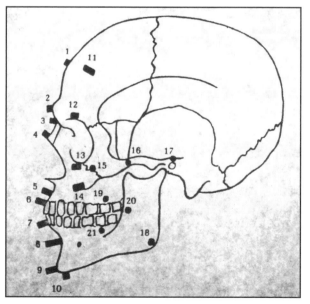

There are 21 points on the skull that have calculated tissue thicknesses. These points are used as reference when creating a reconstructed face.

(Kathleen O. Arries)

unknown person, one that would be so realistic that a wife might recognize her husband or a father might recognize his child? That is the real test.

Bodies are found every year across the country that have no identifying features, no name, and no one comes forward to claim them. The forensic anthropologist examines the bones and writes up the police-blotter description that is sent across the country to other police departments. If no one responds to the police report then a facial reconstruction may be shown to the public in the hope that someone will recognize it.

The Russians have been doing reconstructions since the 1930s and they call it "face finding," which is precisely what it is. It is always a surprise to the artists when they finally see the face that they have been working on.

Finding Frank

In 1981, in Chautauqua County in western New York State, a body was found wrapped up in a sleeping bag. The body was that of a man wearing a denim jacket and jeans with a western-style leather belt hand-tooled with the inscription "Frank." There was no other identification. It was not a pretty sight. Decomposition of the body had been delayed by the sleeping bag and inside it, the remains had liquefied into a putrid brown goo. The face, exposed to the elements was gone, but it was apparent that he had been shot in the head twice. Who was this man?

The county medical examiner viewed the remains, but with no clue as to who they were of, the man would be buried as a John Doe. Kathleen Arries, who consulted with the medical examiner and sheriff's department, pulled the remains from the morgue freezer to see how she could help.

The skull was distinctive. On the left side of the mandible between the chin and jaw, there was a deformation that looked as if a great gouge had been taken out, but the bone had just grown that way. The skull would make a prime candidate for a reconstruction.

Some of the most successful reconstructions are made with skulls that have some distinguishing feature, such as a jutting jaw, a healed trauma that would indicate a noticeable scar during life, or a gold tooth.

Arries noticed markings on the other facial bones that the medical examiner had dismissed as animal teeth marks. A closer look convinced Arries that they were made with a knife. The markings were all parallel, evenly spaced and equally deep, and made at right angles. After killing this man, someone had taken the time to scrape the skin off his face so that he would never be identified. To Arries the case was a challenge that she could not pass up. Reconstructing the dead man's skull would offer him one last chance of being recognized.

Arries preferred to work on a plaster cast of the skull rather than the skull itself. That way the skull is not damaged, and it allows more than one person to work on the skull at the same time. A latex and gauze casting was made and then split off to use as a mold to make a plaster skull.

With the chart listing the reference points and tissue depths specific to adult Caucasian males next to her, Arries began to work. Since Dr. His's discoveries at the turn of the century, researchers have expanded on the data and developed standardized measurements for males and females and the caucasoid, negroid, and mongoloid races.

There are 21 points of the skull for which there are known tissue depths. For each reference point Arries cut a small piece of plasticine to the proper length. The markers, which resemble the eraser at the end of a pencil, are placed on the skull, making it look like an odd form of skeletal acupuncture.

Strips of clay are then placed on the skull connecting the 21 points. Positioning this latticework is like playing connect the dots in three dimensions. The important part is to keep the clay strips the appropriate thickness. As the surrounding areas are filled in and smoothed out, the face begins to take shape.

Eyes were picked out from a small carrying case filled with different size glass eyeballs; blue, green, hazel, and brown, each sitting in a velvet pocket. Arries chose the most common eye color, brown. Contrary to what most people think, eyeballs are pretty much the same size. They grow only slightly from infancy to adulthood. The illusion of big eyes or little eyes is due to the size of the eye opening in the bone called the orbit.

From this point on, Arries had to rely on her art training. Although the bone dictates the contours of the face, it is difficult to determine the shape and size of the nose, the fullness of the lips, and the design of the ears. The underlying bone gives only subtle suggestions about these features, general guidelines that the reconstructionist follows.

The size and shape of the nose is suggested by the size and shape of the nasal opening. The cartilage that supports the tent-like stretch of skin of the nose decays along with the tissue leaving a large triangular-shaped gap. The edge of the opening curves gently outward suggesting where the nose once projected forward. There is a small arrow-shaped bit of bone called the spine that juts out at the base of the nose. It acts as a support and is approximately one-third of the actual length of the nose. In a Caucasian male, the nose is about one-third wider than the nasal opening. Knowing this, Arries could estimate the width and length.

The mouth is roughly as wide as the distance between the pupils of the eyes, but the lips are unpredictable. Arries constructed a generic looking mouth with the lips closed.

The ear is also made of cartilage that decomposes quickly, but estimates on living people show that the ear, from the top to the lobe, is approximately as long as a person's nose. Did the man have dangling earlobes or were they attached? Did his ears stick out or hug the head closely? Again Arries sculpted generic-looking ears.

A reconstruction has to take race into account. For this Caucasian male, Arries sculpted a narrow, long nose and thin lips, but on a negroid skull she would have made the lips a little fuller, and she would have given an Asian male the slight folds over the eyes characteristic of the mongoloid race. Reconstructions may seem to follow stereotypes, but these characteristics have to be considered to get the best result, namely that someone will recognize the unknown person. If the skull belonged to an elderly person, wrinkles and a slight sag of the skin on the neck would have been added for a more authentic appearance.

To create skin texture, fine-grain sandpaper was gently blotted on the smooth clay. The last step was to add hair. Wigs never look completely natural, but they are necessary to the reconstruction process. Arries combed out a man's brown wig that matched the color of a strand of hair found on the skeleton. She photographed the reconstruction for the police to distribute and then added the sunglasses that were found in the dead man's shirt pocket and photographed the reconstructed skull again. No one knows what factor will be crucial in determining the identity of a reconstructed person—it could be as simple as sunglasses.

The police added the reconstruction photos to the homicide file, but no one came forward to identify who they were of. Eleven years later, an informant in Ohio told police about a 10-year-old murder and how the victim was dumped in a field. The circumstances were similar to those surrounding the Chautauqua homicide and the murdered man's name was Frank. Arries's reconstruction helped to corroborate Frank's identification. A state trooper close to the case noted years later that " . . . the reconstruction and drawings were remarkably similar to the man's photograph." On Thursday, October 1, 1992, the district attorney of Chautauqua County issued a statement identifying Frank as a 46-year-old man from Painsville, Ohio, whose body had been dumped in New York. The killer was arrested and convicted, and Frank's remains were returned to his family.

Science and Art

Kathleen Arries had extensive art training that allowed her to reconstruct a skull using clay, but many anthropologists rely on artists who specialize in anatomical and medical drawing to put a face on the bones. Oklahoman Betty Pat Gatliff is an artist who has made a career of medical illustration and sculpting. She was introduced to reconstruction when Clyde Snow, a forensic anthropologist with the state of Oklahoma, presented her with a skull and asked if she could sculpt a face from it. They made a perfect team of science and art. Their first case together was identifying the victims of serial killer John Wayne Gacy.

Gacy was a harmless-looking, middle-aged building contractor, working and living in Des Plaines, Illinois. He was active in the community and even performed as a clown to entertain children at neighborhood events, but that facade quickly disappeared when he was arrested for the murder of a young boy in December 1978. Following information that Gacy himself told them, police discovered the bodies of 16 young boys buried under Gacy's house and garage, and more than 20 others elsewhere. Gacy would not name his victims, so it fell to forensic anthropologists and odontologists to identify them. Dental X rays identified some but progress was slow. All of the victims were the same sex and roughly the same age with little to distinguish them. After a year, nine bodies were still unidentified.

Clyde Snow called Betty Gatliff. Reconstructions were made, photographed, and sent to police stations across the country, printed in newspapers, and viewed on television but no one came forward to identify the boys. Several years went by and Snow and Gatliff had moved on to other cases and forgotten about the nine reconstructions, but one local newspaper reporter had not. Years later, using a photo of a reconstruction, the reporter tracked down the identification of one of the boys, but the other eight were buried unknown.

Grinner—A Face from the Past

In 1987, an unmarked cemetery was uncovered during the construction of a new house on the shores of Lake Erie in Canada. It turned out that the site had once been a burial ground for dead soldiers during the War of 1812. An archaeological team was assigned the job of recovering the bodies and identifying them as

THE RECONSTRUCTION

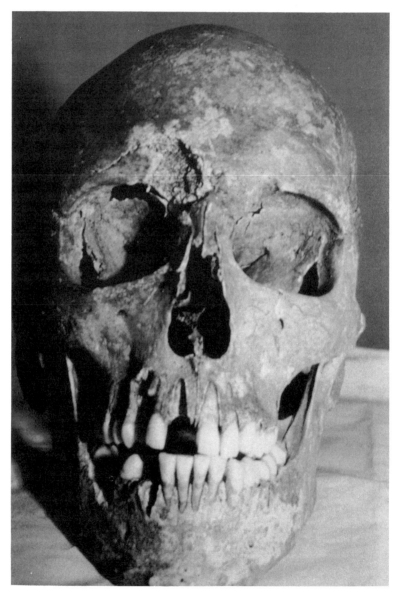

Grinner's skull cleaned and ready for reconstruction.
(Kathleen O. Arries)

The skull is covered in latex and gauze to make a mold.
(Kathleen O. Arries)

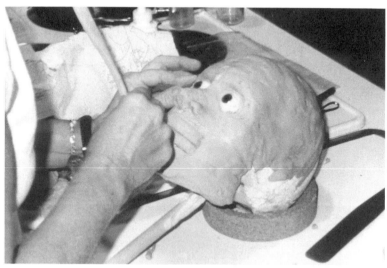

Strips of clay are placed on the mold and smoothed out.
(Kathleen O. Arries)

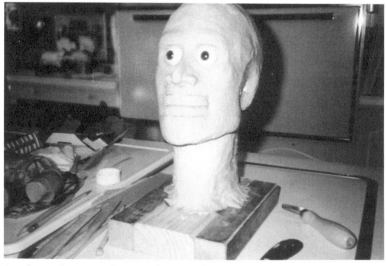

Applying the nose, lips, and ears takes an artist's touch.
(Kathleen O. Arries)

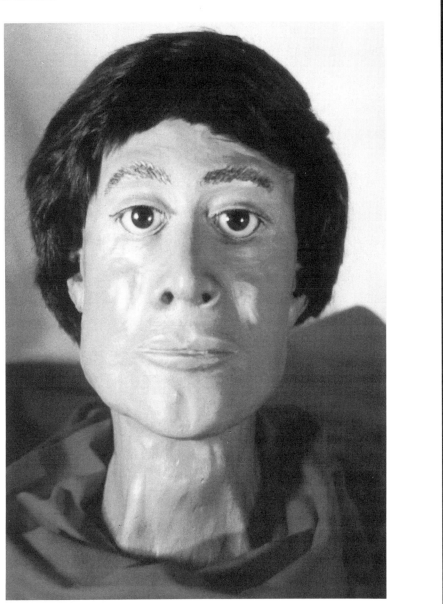

The finished reconstruction of Grinner as he might have looked
before his death in 1812. (Kathleen O. Arries)

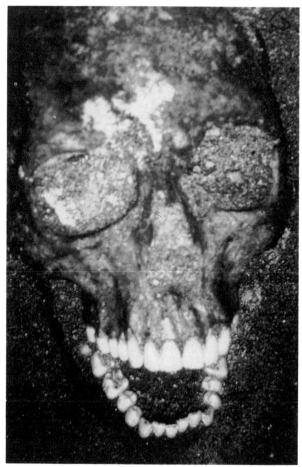

A War of 1812 soldier excavated from his grave. The slackened jaw earned him the nickname Grinner. (Kathleen O. Arries)

best they could. Twenty-eight skeletons were exhumed and from the insignias on the buttons found among the bones it appeared that they were American soldiers. Each skeleton showed signs of battle injuries or medical treatment such as musket fire, cannon blasts, and amputation.

The second soldier to be uncovered had a full set of teeth that gleamed white against the dark brown dirt, and as it is with all skeletons, after the ligaments of the jaw decayed, his heavy mandible dropped to the chest giving him a gaping grin. The archaeological team nicknamed him Grinner.

Grinner had been buried with his feet bound and hands folded across his stomach. Under his right shoulder blade was a copper pin that may have held closed a bandage, suggesting that Grinner had been in a military hospital before he died.

Of all of the skeletons, Grinner's skull was in the best shape; some of the other skulls had been destroyed by cannon fire or were missing altogether. Grinner was a good candidate for a reconstruction. The anthropologist chose to give Grinner blue eyes and reddish brown hair because U.S. Army records indicated that these were the most common features among the soldiers at that time. Now visitors to Fort Erie, Canada, can actually see the face of one of the soldiers who slept in the barracks, stood guard in the towers, and fought and died in the War of 1812.

Museums all over the world use reconstructions to put faces on the past. At a reconstructed Norse village in York, England, there is a reconstruction of a Viking man who lived 1,000 years ago, and at the New York State Museum in Albany, New York, there are reconstructions of early Native Americans depicting what life was like in America long before Europeans arrived.

Perhaps the most intriguing reconstructions are the ones at the American Museum of Natural History in New York City. In the Hall of Human Biology and Evolution there are dioramas that depict early man and woman as they may have looked walking across an African plain more than 3 million years ago. Inspired by a set of footprints found in 1976 that had been fossilized in the mud for 3 million years, paleoanthropologists at the museum speculated about how the ancestors who left those tracks might have looked. Because the couple did not trip and fall into the mud leaving facial impressions, the scientists had to rely on skeletal data such as the 4-foot-tall skeleton known as "Lucy," and other fragments of 3-million-year-old skulls as models for the reconstruction.

10
∇

PHOTOGRAPHIC SUPERIMPOSITION

*C*lay reconstructions are made when the police have no clue as to the identity of a skeleton, but sometimes the police do have an idea who the person may turn out to be, because of unsolved missing person cases or from a passenger list from a crashed airplane. In such instances they are able to determine identity using high-tech photography called *superimposition*, which compares a photograph of the suspected missing person with a skull thought to belong to him or her.

Superimposition is done by using two video cameras that are connected by a cable to a mixer, which is an editing machine that can move the images on and off screen, make them clearer, or fade them out. The skull is mounted vertically on a pedestal or horizontally on a table and positioned at the same angle as the head in the photograph. One video camera is focused on the skull, and the second video camera is focused on the photo.

The mixer is connected to a VCR that plays the images of the skull and the photograph on a television monitor. The mixer can produce the effect of a split screen where a line runs horizontally or vertically between both images at the same time, or half of each image. The line can be moved to show more of one image and less of another across the screen. This is called a wipe. A fade is like a dream sequence in a movie, one image blurs and fades to expose the other image. The fade can be equalized so that you can see both the portrait and the skull as if the person's skin were transparent.

There are many points on the skull that can be compared with the photo to prove that they are of the same person. Each spot must match up exactly in order to prove identity. If even one point on the skull is misaligned the police have to resume their search.

Starting at the bottom of the skull, the center of the jawbone must match up with the point of the chin. The bite line of the teeth on the skull should be even with the lip line on the photograph. The nasal opening should be the same shape and length as the actual nose. Working upward, the position of the eyeballs is checked, they should be centered in the orbits. At the outside of the eye on the outer margin there is a muscle attachment that you can feel by running your finger up the side of your eye socket. Feel at the top where the bone abruptly turns toward the back of the head. On some people this line is visible and can be matched with the bone structure on the skull. The small opening of the ear canal on the skull should align with the ear canal as observed in the photograph.

Video equipment used for superimposition. The monitor in the center blends the photographic image on the left with the image of the skull on the right.
(William R. Maples)

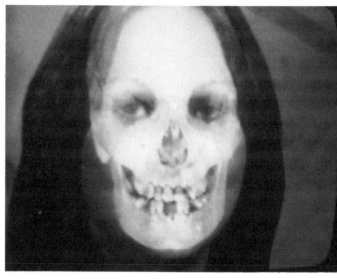
The eerie image of a skull superimposed on a photograph of a woman. The points of reference match up exactly. (William R. Maples)

The best kind of photograph to use for superimposition is one in which the person is smiling. William Maples, of the C.A. Pound Human ID Laboratory of the Florida Museum of Natural History at the University of Florida points out that a person's teeth are unique because of all the dental irregularities and imperfections we all possess. If Maples gets a match on the teeth, he needs only to do a spot check to see that all the rest matches up.

Aging in an adult does not affect the identification process at all. As we get older, earlobes lengthen, the tip of the nose droops, wrinkles crease the forehead and the area around the eyes, and the skin loosens and sags, but all this happens on the surface. The inner bone structure remains the same. However, children's facial bones are changing and growing so rapidly that superimposition is less accurate for them. Superimposition would not work, for example, using a photo taken of a child at 10 years of age if that child died at age 15.

Case of the Missing Prison Guard

Photography played a major role in identifying the body of a North Carolina correctional officer who had been missing for four years.

A partial skeleton was found in a rural area of scrub brush and woods, and an initial examination of it concluded that it was of a Caucasian man, about 30 years old and approximately 5 feet 7 inches tall. According to the medical examiner's report the man had been dead more than two years but less than 10. Gunshot wounds on the skeleton pointed to the cause of death. This description fit that of the missing prison guard, and police contacted his family for X rays or other material that would help confirm his identity. The family had nothing but a close-up photograph taken of the man at his high school graduation. Needing more information, the police contacted local dentists to see if any of them had worked on the officer's teeth. No one had. Identification had to result from the photo.

The forensic anthropologist on the case aligned the skull in the exact same position as the head in the portrait and superimposed the images of the graduation photo and skull on the television monitor. Fortunately in the photo the man was smiling and the teeth matched perfectly, right down to the overlap of the incisors on the neighboring teeth, and the chip in the front tooth. The missing prison guard had been found.

Mitch Boyer

General George Armstrong Custer led the Seventh Calvary during the Battle of Little Bighorn against the Sioux and Cheyenne, and he died on what is now called Custer Hill at Custer's Last Stand on June 2, 1876. More than 267 soldiers and civilians died on the plains that day, along with many Sioux and Cheyenne. There were no survivors from the U.S. Army to tell about the events of the battle. When troops arrived days later, the bodies they found strewn across the hills were buried where they lay.

Over 100 years bones from those graves have been uncovered by brush fire, pushed up by heaving frost, and dug up by archaeologists. Most of the bones were fragmented and scattered. In 1985, Clyde Snow took an interest in the osteobiographies of the soldiers on the hill and went to the battlefield to see if any of the remains could be identified. One small fragment only 4 inches long and 2 inches wide looked promising. It was the upper jawbone with eight teeth still intact. The nasal opening was not characteristically caucasoid as Snow would have suspected the soldier to be. It was mongoloid shaped, which indicated that maybe the man was a Sioux or Cheyenne, but the teeth were not shovel shaped as mongoloid teeth usually are. It was a puzzle. Snow checked through the historical records and came up with one man, Mitch Boyer, who was an interpreter and scout for Custer's men. Boyer's father was

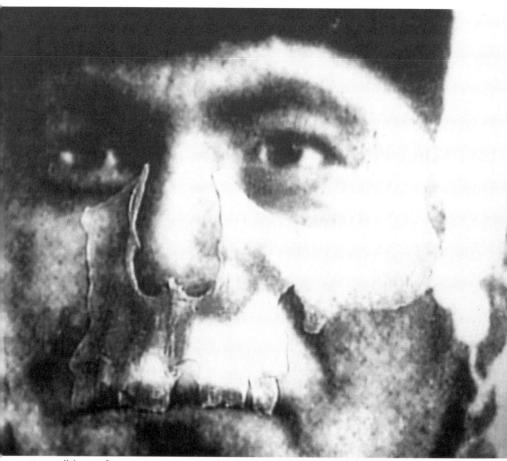

A small bone fragment was more than enough to match with a photograph of Mitch Boyer, one of Custer's scouts. (Midwest Archeological Center, National Park Service)

∇

French and his mother was Santee Sioux, which would explain the mix in racial characteristics. In the historical records there was a photograph that could be used for a superimposition. The skull fragment was small, but it offered a lot for comparison, and the pieces fit. The nasal opening lined up with the nose, the eyes sat in the middle of the eye socket, and the lips and teeth lined up perfectly. Snow had made a 100-year-old match.

Bones, Bullets, and Bank Robbers

Today photographic equipment is used to match more than just skulls to faces. Radiographs, which are enhanced X rays, taken during a person's life can be superimposed with radiographs taken of bones after death. Small hairline fractures, abnormalities in the bone, signs of disease, and evidence of surgery can be compared to confirm identification.

Some of William Maples's work doesn't even include the dead. Maples has been able to compare photographs of robbers taken during a bank hold-up by surveillance cameras to mug shots of suspects. One case involving the security cameras at an automatic teller machine proved a man's innocence. The police had arrested someone for the crime, but when Maples compared the suspect's photo with that taken by the bank cameras, they did not match. The police discovered they had the wrong man and let him go.

Another case involved photographs of a dental implant. A Florida woman who died of natural causes had requested in her will that she be cremated. She was, but the family believed that the crematorium had mishandled her remains and had not put their loved one in the proper place. The family brought a law suit.

At the time of death, the woman had a dental post, a screw-like device that holds a crown set in the mouth. A dental post was also among the ashes. Maples decided to try to match a photograph of the dental post with X rays from the woman's dentist. They matched line for line and dent for dent. The crematorium had done nothing wrong and the case was dropped.

Maples and his staff work on 70 to 120 forensic cases a year, but only three or four of them require the use of superimposition. It is used as a last resort when fingerprinting and X rays are not available.

A student of William Maples's conducted a study to determine the reliability of using superimposition to determine a perfect match. She took 100 mug shots of criminals and superimposed each one onto three totally unrelated skulls. She found that in eight cases she was able to make a match of the skull with the photograph in one view, the front view matched up but the side view did not, or the side view matched up but the front view did not. In only one case did she find a match in both views. In 99 percent of the cases a match on more than one photograph would mean a positive identification. It also demonstrated the need for scientists to use more than one method of identification. None of the methods is 100 percent accurate.

Some agencies such as the FBI use computers rather than the two-camera method and eyeballing it, as Maples does. He warns against the manipulation that computers are programmed to do. In a recent experiment, a photograph of George Bush was gradually enhanced and manipulated until it turned into a portrait of Bill Clinton. As Maples points out, a computer is programmed to make adjustments and those adjustments might mistakenly match a photograph to a skull.

The big advance in photographic forensic work is not in the technology but in the application. Photography will be used more often in the courtroom. Until now jurors have had to sit through the long-winded and technical speeches of expert witnesses, but now forensic anthropologists can use video equipment to let the jurors see for themselves how a skull fits the photograph of a woman or how the bowing of the femur in an X ray taken of the victim matches exactly the bowing in the femur of a skeleton found in a garbage dump.

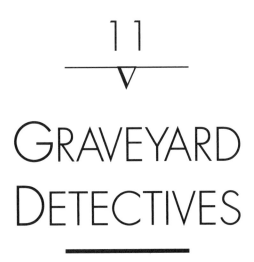

11

GRAVEYARD DETECTIVES

𝒥osef Mengele was a medical doctor and a high-ranking Nazi officer in Adolf Hitler's army during World War II. To many he is also known as the "Angel of Death," because Mengele was responsible for the deaths of more than 400,000 people at Auschwitz, the largest death camp in the Nazi regime. At Auschwitz, Mengele performed ghoulish tortures on the inmates, experimenting on them to prove his twisted theories of the superiority of the Aryan race.

On January 27, 1945, when the Russian Army marched into Auschwitz they found the camp empty of life. All that was left were smoldering furnaces and thousands of dead bodies. The Angel of Death had slipped away and vanished, and the search for the most wanted war criminal began.

Nazi hunters followed every lead and checked every rumor, tracking Mengele across countries and over continents, and each time they came up empty. For 40 years after the liberation of Auschwitz, the search continued. In 1985, a new clue surfaced that led Nazi hunters to a grave in the hills of Embú, Brazil, and a woman named Lisolette Bossert. Bossert told the police that in 1979 she had arranged for the burial of a friend named Wolfgang Gerhard and that Gerhard had drowned in a swimming accident. But after hours of interrogation Bossert admitted that the man in the grave was not Gerhard, but Mengele. Wolfgang Gerhard had really been an Austrian and a friend to both Bossert and Mengele. In 1971, Gerhard had decided to return to Austria, but before he did, he gave Mengele his Brazilian identification card. Mengele's photograph was inserted onto it, giving him a new identity. Prior to that he had used the name Peter Hochbichler. It was believed that Mengele had been found.

The discovery of Josef Mengele was of worldwide importance. He was a major war criminal, and if he was still alive he could be tried for his crimes against humanity. And if he was dead, many people could put their minds to rest knowing that the mystery was over.

Quickly news of the discovery spread. The governments of Brazil, the United States, and West Germany sent teams of forensic scientists to São Paulo, Brazil, to study the remains. An independent team from the Wiesenthal Center in California acting on behalf of many Jewish Americans was also sent. One of the top forensic anthropologists, Clyde Snow, was on the team.

There was one body (called the Embú skeleton) with two possible identities. It could not yet be ruled out that Bossert's story was another attempt to throw authorities off Mengele's track. The possibility that the skeleton could be Gerhard's had to be checked. Before looking at the bones, the first item of business was gathering information about the physical characteristics of Gerhard from medical and government records, and of Mengele from German secret service reports, dental charts, photographs, and personal interviews. This information would be compared to the skeletal data.

Next, each forensic team got to look at the remains, each scientist pouring over them, attacking the project from his own specialty. The skull had been badly smashed by a gravedigger's shovel, and many of the pieces were no bigger than a dime. It would have to be reconstructed. German anthropologist Richard Helmer, a skull expert, took on the job. The rest of the teams took turns measuring and analyzing the various bones.

The first question to be answered was whether the skeleton was male or female? The head of the femur, and the head of the humerus were large, the jaw was square and robust, and the pelvis narrow. The experts all agreed that the Embú skeleton was that of a male.

After several days Helmer was finished with the skull reconstruction. The shape of the face indicated that the man was Caucasian.

To get the man's height the femur was measured. When the man was alive he stood 173.5 centimeters, or 5 feet, 8 inches tall. That ruled out the real Gerhard. Information collected on Gerhard indicated that he was taller. In fact, Gerhard had a German nickname, Langer. In the United States he would have been called Stretch. According to the German S.S. reports, Mengele was 174 centimeters tall.

The bones were from a man between 60 and 70 years old. Information on Gerhard indicated that he was only 50 when he died. Dr. Ellis Kerley, who devised the microscopic bone analysis for determining age, sliced a wafer thin section of the femur. Under the microscope he determined that the man had died in his late sixties.

From the shoulder blade and shoulder socket, scientists discovered that the Embú skeleton had been right-handed. So was Mengele, but so are most people. So far the teams had found nothing that refuted the possibility that the man in the grave was Josef Mengele, but they still did not have conclusive proof.

X rays taken of Mengele before he died would have been very useful. They are like fingerprints; no two people's X rays are alike. But there were no dental X rays to be found. Mengele was believed to have lived in Brazil for many years, and the teeth on the skeleton showed signs of dental work. There had to have been a dentist somewhere who had worked on these teeth.

Meanwhile, Helmer, who in Germany had perfected the technique of video-imaging a photograph on a skull, was ready to compare the skull with a photograph of Mengele. If the skull was indeed that of Josef Mengele, it would match up with the photograph point by point. If it did not, then it was somebody else buried in that grave. Helmer stuck markers on the skull to correspond with the known tissue thicknesses. Then he focused a video camera on the skull, and one on a photograph of Mengele in his Nazi uniform. The forensic teams were gathered together in the photography room, all eyes fixed on the television monitor where the image of Mengele appeared and then the ghostly image of the skull appeared beneath it. Each marker seemed to touch the filmy image of the skin as if it was holding it up from inside. Every point matched.

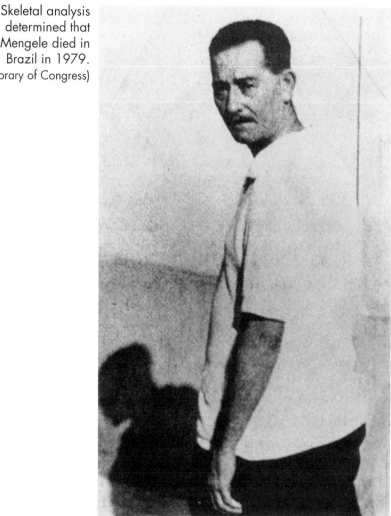

Skeletal analysis determined that Mengele died in Brazil in 1979. (Library of Congress)

The video image convinced everyone in that room that the man in the grave was indeed Mengele—but that was not good enough proof. The teams' responsibility was to use physical evidence to prove beyond any doubt the identity of the man, so the dental X rays were still needed.

After more searching and interviews, a dentist in a distant Brazilian village admitted to working on a man named Gerhard in 1978. Pointing him out in a photograph, he pointed directly to Mengele. The dentist handed over the X rays in his file. The dental X rays were superimposed with X rays taken of the teeth in the Embú skull, which had already been accurately superimposed with Mengele's photograph. If the Gerhard X rays matched the skull, then it would prove that the man who called himself Gerhard in 1978 was really Josef Mengele. The X rays matched perfectly right down to the gap between the two front teeth, which was one of Mengele's more striking features.

Each team felt that they had proven without a doubt that the body in the grave was Josef Mengele who had been living quietly in Brazil under an assumed identity of Wolfgang Gerhard. For the Brazilian, U.S., and German governments and the Wiesenthal team, the case of the most wanted murderer was closed. Israel has still not issued a formal statement about Mengele's death. To many Jews who were tortured and whose families were killed, it is still an open wound.

Graveyard Detectives

History is being rewritten by forensic scientists who try to solve some of the biggest mysteries that have captured the attention of the American public for decades, such as the disappearance of pilot Amelia Earhart. Earhart flew out over the Pacific on July 2, 1937, on the last leg of what would have been her world-record flight around the equator, but she was never seen again. Somewhere between New Guinea and Howland Island her plane went down. Neither her plane nor her remains have ever been found, although people still search for her. Some bones and teeth uncovered from an unmarked grave in Micronesia promised to be the real thing, until anthropologists proved them to be the remains of an elderly male islander. So, the search still continues.

One anthropologist, James Starrs of George Washington University, is an avid graveyard sleuth. He has exhumed the body of Meriwether Lewis of the Lewis and Clark Expedition who supposedly committed suicide. Starrs wanted to see if perhaps it was murder, but the bones did not reveal anything conclusive. He also examined the victims of Alfred Packer, an alleged cannibal, to see if this charge was true. It was, the bodies all showed signs of butcher marks. Another case he reexamined was that of Carl Weiss, a doctor who allegedly killed Louisiana governor Huey Long in 1935.

According to the official records of the incident, Weiss confronted Long in the state capitol building where Weiss drew his gun and shot Long in the stomach. Long's bodyguards reacted by shooting Weiss many times. This official version was never questioned, although other facts contradicted it. In the hospital, Long was reported to have said that he got a split lip where Weiss hit him with his fist, and one of the bodyguards was overheard lamenting about having killed his own boss.

These discrepancies peaked Starrs's curiosity. With the permission of his family Weiss's body was exhumed and examined. Weiss's body had been riddled with at least 23 bullets shot by the governor's bodyguards from all sides, half from the back, seven from the front, and five from the side. The scene had been chaotic. From the trajectory of the bullet wounds, it seems highly probable that Huey Long could have been hit by a stray bullet fired from the gun of one of his own bodyguards rather than by Weiss. Starrs's examination does not alter the facts, but does raise questions about the long-accepted official version.

In order to exhume a body Starrs, like all forensic anthropologists, has to get permission from the deceased's family and a court order. Starrs is currently waiting for permission to exhume the bodies of Lizzie Borden's father and stepmother to see if Lizzie Borden really took an axe and gave her mother 40 whacks. But the work Starrs does is controversial in the forensic field. Many people believe that exhuming the dead is a violation of a sacred resting place and the historic cases are sensationalized to feed the public's morbid curiosity.

Many forensic anthropologists think there should be limits and controls placed on who gets to exhume the dead and for what purpose. In the future, a panel of experts may be established to set down guidelines for exhumations and testing. Bodies would be reexamined only for reasons of great importance rather than idle curiosity.

One case where exhumation proved to be necessary was the case of slain civil rights leader Medgar Evers. Bryon de la Beckwith, the man accused of murdering Evers, stood trial twice. Both times the juries were deadlocked, and Beckwith went free. Twenty-nine years later the case was reopened, but the original autopsy report was missing. Evers was exhumed in order to conduct a new autopsy.

Is there anyone Starrs would not reexamine? Yes. He, like many other forensic experts would not exhume John F. Kennedy. Not only would there be little to learn from the examination, but, Starrs says, it would be like exhuming his father.

On the Outlaw Trail

Clyde Snow enjoys going after the bad guys, especially when they are already dead. When he was presented with the mystery of Robert Leroy Parker and Harry A. Longabaugh, better known as Butch Cassidy and the Sundance Kid, he was excited to join the chase.

Butch and Sundance were two of the most notorious, elusive, and romanticized outlaws of the wild west, staying one step ahead of the law before finally fleeing to South America in the early 1900s. From there the story gets muddled and mythical. Did they settle down and become cattle ranchers in Bolivia or did they come back to the United States as some stories claim? Were they buried in a remote village in Bolivia after being gunned down by Bolivian army soldiers? Snow hoped to solve the mystery once and for all, but first he needed ammunition: papers and reports about the outlaws' physical characteristics and medical condition. Snow found what he was looking for in old prison records and Pinkerton detective reports. Armed with this information, Snow and a team of historians, archaeologists, and forensic researchers set off for the dusty mining town of San Vincente, Bolivia.

San Vincente lies 15,000 feet above sea level high in the Andes. Snow described the landscape as so sparse the buzzards had to pack a lunch. On the outskirts of town, surrounded by a tall mud-brick wall was a cemetery. Inside the wall was a sea of tombstones and wooden crosses; new graves mingled with the old. In the middle of the maze, under a small block of stone that had long since lost its plaque and cross, the two outlaws were said to have been buried.

Butch and Sundance's last heist was robbing a courier carrying a mining company's payroll. The courier collected three Bolivian army soldiers who tracked the outlaws to San Vincente where they had rented a room for the night. As the soldiers approached the sun-dried brick house, they saw Butch and Sundance's rifles leaning against the wall by the door. The soldiers ordered the outlaws to come out. The records are confused as to who shot first, but the official record from the Bolivian army states that the two men ran out into the courtyard where the shorter outlaw (Butch) shot the other in the forehead and then turned the gun on himself, committing suicide. The two were buried in the village cemetery.

Two tall European-looking North Americans in a cemetery full of shorter, more compact South Americans should be easy to pick out, but Snow and his team discovered a problem. A Swedish miner, who shot himself accidentally while trying to get down off his mule, and a German prospector, who blew himself up while thawing frozen dynamite in an oven, were also buried somewhere in the cemetery. There would be a chance of digging them up instead of the outlaws.

The exhumation began after a local shaman gave an offering of cigarettes and alcohol to appease the spirits for disturbing the grave site. The first bones found were loose stray bones from older graves that had been moved to make room for newer ones, a common practice where space is limited. Digging further, they found what they were looking for, a complete skeleton. The coffin

The Hole-in-the-Wall Gang. Sundance is seated on the far left, and Butch on the far right. (Union Pacific Railroad Company)

had disintegrated leaving only stray nails every few inches. They found buttons similar to those on a denim jacket and a belt buckle. The skull was lifted out for Snow to inspect. He turned it in his hands and declared it to be a Caucasian male. The mandible was hoisted up next. From the teeth, Snow estimated the age between 30 and 40 years old. Snow had seen so many bones that a quick look was enough to tell him that they were on the right track, "Like anything else, the more you do a job the better you get," he said.

After two days of digging, only one skeleton was uncovered. The remains were taken back to the United States where a team of experts, a microscopist, forensic odontologist, podiatrist, and radiologist would add to the story. An anthropologist seldom works alone. The most thorough investigation requires a multi-disciplinary approach.

The microscopist examined the the buttons and belt buckles for any identifying marks or inscriptions. They were made in the United States at the turn of the century. The radiologist x-rayed the bones, looking for metal fragments from bullet wounds and traces of healed broken bones.

The scientists met to pool their research, listing their discoveries on a chalk board. Was the skeleton found in the San Vincente grave Butch? No, the skeleton was too tall for it to be Butch, and a superimposition of the skull with a photograph taken of Butch at the Wyoming prison in 1894 did not correspond at all.

Their hopes were pinned on Sundance. The skull's head injury corresponded with the written reports of Sundance having been shot in the head, but the damage to the skull made it difficult to superimpose the skull with a photograph. Some of the reference points lined up, but not enough of the skull was present to make identification conclusive. In forensics there is no room for reasonable doubt.

A podiatrist looked at the leg and foot bones and the remains of the shoes. He discovered that the person would have walked with an unusual gait, because of the angle of the bones. The historian pointed out that Sundance had another nickname "the Straddler," because he walked bowlegged and with a limp. Snow wondered if this condition was hereditary and tracked down Sundance's distant relatives, the Longaboughs, in Pennsylvania. The males in the family all walked slightly bowlegged because of the way their toes curled up. That was one piece of evidence that strongly suggested the skeleton was Sundance.

The radiologist showed the other scientists the X rays that revealed some shrapnel in the cranium that would be consistent with a bullet in the head, but there was no sign of a healed gunshot wound that Sundance was reported to have had.

The last step in identifying the skeleton was to try to match samples of DNA from the bones, with samples of DNA from Sundance's nearest blood relative, a member of the Longabough family. The DNA did not match. Whoever the man in the cemetery was it was neither Butch nor Sundance.

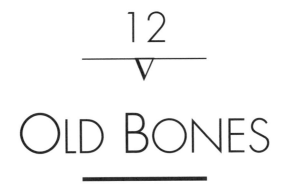

12
OLD BONES

*M*urder and mayhem are not the full-time occupations of most forensic anthropologists. Many are curators at museums or professors at universities, concentrating on ancient mysteries dug from the ground of archaeological sites.

More than a hundred years ago, archaeologists routinely tossed ancient human remains into the garbage pile after the funerary decorations made of gold and precious gems were stripped from them. As a source of information, bones were largely ignored. What little analysis was being done was conducted by paleoanthropologists searching for early humans. Often their conclusions were wrong, for example, categorizing gorilla and chimpanzee bones as the "missing link" between humans and their earlier primate ancestors. One of the first Neandertal skeletons to be discovered in a French cave in 1908 near La Chapelle-aux-Saints was badly disfigured by arthritis. The long bones were bowed and the vertebral column was bent, but scientists, excited by such a find, labeled it typical for that species. Since then, most illustrations in books and magazines mistakenly portray Neandertals as hunched-backed, stoop-shouldered, ape-like creatures, even though scientists have since learned they walked as erect as modern humans.

Today, physical anthropologists and paleoanthropologists view bones from ancient burial grounds as the key to understanding past populations as a whole, rather than focusing on the individual and his or her identity as in forensics. The data taken from many individuals is compiled to illustrate the changes that have occurred over time, for instance, human skull size is steadily increasing. The focus may be different, but the methods are the same—bone analysis, dental examinations, blood and tissue tests, and non-invasive medical technology.

Non-invasive Analysis

Ancient bone reveals as much as more recent bones examined in forensic work. The activities people performed molded their skeletal framework. For example, King Henry VIII's archers habitually pulled back on a taut bow string causing an extra bony deposit to form at the tip of the shoulder, making the shoulder blade forked. An Egyptian scribe's long hours of writing caused marked lines of attachment to form, which supported enlarged muscles on the right hand. The legs became bowed from long hours of sitting cross-legged on the floor with a skirt stretched tautly over the knees serving as a desk.

Bone analysis is revealing, but in order to examine the bones of a mummy, for example, it has to be unwrapped. The Egyptian government has restricted access to the remains of ancient pharaohs so it has become necessary to utilize other methods to "see" into

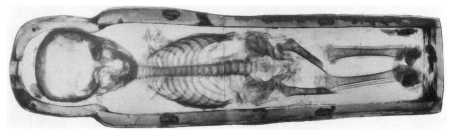

An X ray of an Egyptian mummified infant shows a curved spine and broken legs. (The Field Museum, Neg#59105, Chicago)

the body without damaging it, using technology borrowed from modern medicine. Simple X rays have revealed animal remains inside coffins where human remains were expected to be, and, in some cases, more than one individual in a coffin. A radiograph, which is a blend of an X ray and a photocopy, shows soft tissue as well as bone on the same image. A radiograph taken of the head of Egyptian pharaoh Ramesses II revealed for the first time a tiny animal bone placed inside the nose and behind it a cluster of beads.

CAT (computerized axial tomography) scans are another way to view the inside of a body without destroying the outside. The body is slid into the scanner's large cylindrical chamber. It scans the body and takes a cross-sectional X ray at intervals as small as a half a millimeter. The "slices" can be combined to produce a three-dimensional image of the inside of the body that is viewed on a monitor. The scanner registers soft tissues as well as bone material and has been used to identify 4,000-year-old parasites and tumors.

Fiberoptic endoscopes, which are miniature cameras with a light source mounted on small flexible tubing, are placed inside body cavities to inspect the contents. A fiberoptic scope was inserted into the skull of a 2,000-year-old body found in a peat bog and showed that the brain, which appeared to be present on CAT scans, had deteriorated to a mass of putty-like tissue.

Trace Elements

After viewing the remains, a more detailed analysis of the bone's components is called for. The major chemical elements in bone are calcium, phosphorus, oxygen, carbon, nitrogen, and hydrogen, but bone also contains chemicals found in such small amounts that they are called trace elements. Some trace elements such as copper, manganese, iodine, and zinc, are necessary for the human body to work properly, but other trace elements, such as mercury, lead, and arsenic, are not essential and can be toxic in large amounts. These elements get into the body through ingestion, inhalation, and absorption through the skin, and they stay in the bone long after death. Each element has many isotopes, which are variations of an element. The atoms of the same chemical element can have different weights and properties due to the number of neutrons in the nucleus. Certain isotopes are specific to geographic regions, and by measuring the amount of a certain isotope that is found in the bone, scientists can determine what kind of foods the person ate, where he or she may have lived, and the toxicity of the environment.

Strontium is an element found in soil that is absorbed into our bodies and particularly into teeth, where thick dental enamel covers and preserves it. Plant-eaters retain more strontium than meat-eaters do and omnivores such as humans who eat both meat and plants have an intermediate level of strontium. Early hominid fossils of *Australopithicus robustus* were tested for strontium, and the results indicated that these particular early ancestors were strictly vegetarians.

To identify what type of isotope exists in a bone sample, scientists use mass spectrometry, which measures the atomic weight of the isotope. By matching the strontium isotopes in teeth with the strontium in soil samples, scientists can locate the source of the food.

To identify an ancient person's origins, similar tests are conducted to identify the oxygen isotopes absorbed into the human body from drinking water. For example, a person who spent his or her life drinking rainwater from the South American tropical rain forest will have a different isotope concentration than a person who spent his or her life drinking rainwater that fell on the arctic.

Analyzing bone for lead tells us that lead poisoning was common throughout the ages. Romans had high lead levels from ingesting it from wine vessels and cooking utensils and absorbing it through the skin from women's cosmetics. Lead levels in early American colonists reveal class distinctions. Only the wealthiest people who could afford pewter containers and glazed pottery were poisoning themselves with lead. The poor did not have such high levels in their bones.

▽

Family Ties

Ancient bone retains small amounts of blood proteins, such as albumin and hemoglobin, that can be detected by a test called ELISA (enzyme-linked immunosorbent assay), which identifies a specific protein by linking it with an antibody. ELISA has identified blood proteins in bone that was cremated, in red pigment used in Paleolithic cave paintings, and also in residue on stone tools. Once the protein has been identified, it can be tested for the specific blood groups, such as the A,B,O system, and other more specific sub-groupings that we inherit from our parents.

Royal lineages that have been recorded on ancient bits of papyrus, painted in hieroglyphics, and carved into tomb walls can now be proved by blood tests. Reconstituted blood cells taken from the mummy of Tutankhamen, the boy king who ruled Egypt more than 3,000 years ago, were matched with blood samples from a mummy of an unidentified male who resembled the young pharaoh. Scientists now believe that they have found Smenkhare, Tutankhamen's older brother, or his father, the pharaoh Akhenaten.

The advancements in genetics and DNA have opened up many possibilities for working out familial relationships between individuals and for mapping human migration. DNA that was extracted from a 7,000-year-old skull found in Florida revealed an unknown DNA sequence that is not found in DNA samples taken from the present population, suggesting that this individual's lineage probably died out a long time ago. Mapping the genes from modern-day Native Americans has revealed three distinct groupings, and scientists believe that this translates into three major waves of ancient people crossing the Bering Strait and populating different parts of the Americas.

Ancient Disease

One of the approaches of physical anthropology is to look at the health of a population to gain insight into what was happening in that community. The sudden presence of disease might reflect recent change such as contact with an outside culture or difficulty coping with the environment. The contact between the Native American populations and Europeans, for example, was not a healthy one. It is a controversial subject, but many archaeologists believe that some European diseases, such as tuberculosis and syphilis, were spread throughout the Native American population. In its advanced stage syphilis affects the bone, leaving it porous and full of holes, and bones affected with syphilis are not found in ancient Native American burial sites until after European contact.

Not all diseases affect bone. Some like cholera and the plague kill so quickly that there are no skeletal changes. The most common disorders found in ancient skeletons are fractures, arthritis, bone infections, and dental disease, all still common complaints of today, and just like today many of the common diseases did not kill. For example, in ancient Egypt it was very common to have extremely bad teeth. They were worn down from a lifetime of eating course grains made coarser by wind blown sand in the diet. Silicosis, a disease of the lungs caused by breathing in sand and dust, was also common, along with arthritis and river parasites.

Polio, the terrifying disease that leaves children paralyzed and crippled, has plagued humans around the world for centuries. Carvings and drawings on an Egyptian tomb dating back 3,000 years, suggest that the pharaoh Siptah was inflicted with polio, and the bones inside the linen wrappings bear this out. The pharaoh's muscles had atrophied, or weakened, and his foot had become so deformed that it stretched to compensate for the shortened leg. Now scientists know that polio is even older than this. Australian archaeologists working in the United Arab Emirates on the Persian Gulf uncovered what they believe to be the earliest case of polio, dating back 4,000 years. They found the skeleton of a woman judged to be 18 years old, whose body was so disfigured that she probably could not walk.

Wounds of War

Just as bone analysis allows the forensic anthropologist to reconstruct the events of a murder, physical anthropologists can gauge the violence occuring at a particular site by looking at the wounds present on skeletons found there and determine how they were inflicted. An archaeological excavation of an early "16th" century Native American village revealed a battle with Europeans that was never recorded.

The King site located on the Coosa River in Georgia was a large cultural center for the chiefdom of Coosa complete with strong defensive walls enclosing a large central plaza, ball court, and ceremonial center. Researchers were surprised to uncover many burials at the site that showed violent death. One in every five skeletons had lethal slash wounds on the head and legs. The angle and length of the wounds indicated that they were made by long blades such as European swords, and the head and leg injuries were similar to wounds seen in European soldiers. Spanish soldiers were traditionally trained to attack the head and legs of their foe, because the European soldier's torso was protected by armor, whereas the typical Native American weapon such as the lance and bow and arrow caused piercing wounds to the chest. In battles between Native Americans, it was unusual for warriors ever to kill females. Women were usually captured and adopted into families; however, at this site the victims were mostly young or middle-aged women with only a few middle-aged men wounded in the same manner. There was no evidence of children or young men being injured.

From the evidence, the researchers pieced together this scenario. The only Spanish expedition that would have been in that area at that time was Hernando de Soto's. He and his men must have come upon the village while the Indian warriors were battling their neighbors. The Spanish looted the village and tried to enslave the older men and women and perhaps took them some distance from the village before they were killed. Mice and opossum chew marks on all of the injured bones indicate that the bodies must have lain exposed for some time before they were discovered by the survivors and brought back to the village for burial.

Native American Remains

Native Americans in the United States do not want the remains of their ancestors disturbed. However, for decades archaeologists have been excavating and removing ancient remains, viewing them as a source of information about the past, to be studied and stored in museums and universities. These opposing views have caused many conflicts over particular excavation sites, and it has forced many states to enact laws governing the handling of ancient remains uncovered by construction or archaeological excavation. When a burial is unearthed, the local Native American community leaders are notified and participate in the decisions that are made concerning the site. They have realized that it is better to have archaeologists remove the skeletons intact rather than have a bulldozer come and destroy them. The bones must be examined in order to determine if they are ancient Native American remains or not. At sites where the remains are not immediately threatened by construction the remains can be studied in place and covered again.

For remains of Native Americans that have already been removed from their place of burial, the federal government passed a controversial law in 1990 called the Native American Graves Protection and Repatriation Act. It calls for the return, upon request, of all Native American remains and artifacts currently housed in institutions receiving federal funding. The Smithsonian has already returned 2,000 skeletons and plans to return more. By 1995, all institutions are required to have catalogued the artifacts and notified all Native American groups of their holdings. It is a lengthy process and disputes that arise are mediated by a federal panel of experts.

There are archaeologists who oppose the reburial act, arguing that it will cut off research data and jeopardize the science of archaeology, but Native American groups believe that this law that

∇

grants them the right to govern what happens to their ancestors is long overdue. Some Native American groups do not plan on reburial and will open their own museums in order to have better control over how research is conducted. The future of archaeology in the United States will hinge on compromise and cooperation between the scientific community and the Native American communities.

The Body in the Bog

One of the most extensively studied bodies in the world is a 2,000-year-old body called Lindow Man, dredged from the peat bogs of Lindow Moss in northwest England. Although the lower half of the body is missing, it is obviously that of a man because of its well-preserved beard, moustache, and sideburns. It is also

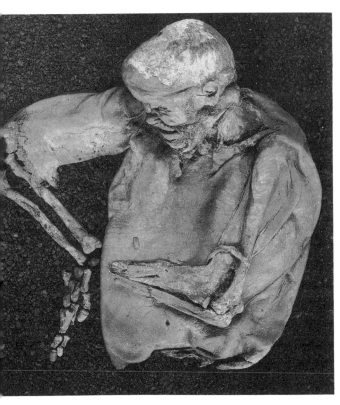

Lindow Man's preserved remains reveal a violent death from stab wounds, slit throat, broken bones, and strangulation.
(Copyright British Museum)

apparent that he had died a violent death. Lindow Man had been struck on the back of the head at least twice by a narrow-bladed weapon, which cut the skin and fractured the skull. He suffered severe blows to his back and chest, breaking a rib and other bones. After he was unconscious, a knotted rope of sinew was tied around his neck strangling him. Finally his throat was slit, severing the jugular vein, and his lifeless body was dropped into the peat bog.

We know what happened to Lindow Man, but we do not know why. Was he sacrificed, or executed for a crime? We do know that he is not unique. Eleven other bodies have been dredged up from bogs all over England—seven men and four women—and they all have multiple wounds in the chest, head fractures, and have been decapitated.

African Burial Ground

The African Burial Ground uncovered in the heart of New York City in 1990 opened up an opportunity to conduct one of the largest osteological studies on a culture that many people have long forgotten. Most people do not realize that the labor of slaves built New York City. In 1664 when the Dutch ceded Manhattan to the British, African slaves made up 40 percent of the population. The British imported 6,000 more Africans between 1700 and 1774. New York was a thriving, bustling port; at the time, it had the largest number of enslaved Africans of any English colony, second only to Charleston, South Carolina. But little is known of this population that built and worked in New York in the 18th century.

In 1697, New York City forbade slaves to bury their dead in Lower Manhattan, so the African population built cemeteries outside city limits. Today that burial ground is a short two blocks north of City Hall. As the city expanded around and eventually over the old cemetery, it was forgotten, until 1990 when a new federal building was planned for that site. When new construction is proposed, an archaeological survey has to be done to check if the site is a culturally significant one. The survey showed that the site had originally been a cemetery, but it was believed that earlier construction had destroyed it. This was not the case. Within the first days of digging, bones were uncovered, halting construction. Approximately 400 burials were recovered. The skeletons provide the largest sample of Africans in America in the 18th century and will provide vital information about their lives at that time.

The bones of all 400 individuals are currently being cleaned, restored, and reconstructed in the Anthropological Lab at Howard University in Washington, D.C. The process will take years to complete and has three main goals. The first is to reconstruct the population, that is, determine their genetic and cultural affiliation. By looking at artifacts and comparing blood samples, researchers hope to be able to classify the individuals specifically as Ashanti, Irish, or Native American, rather than just as caucasoid, negroid, and mongoloid. Blood samples and DNA extracts will be tested and compared with samples from today's living populations. Teeth and cusp patterns, which are the arrangements of the bumps on the grinding surface of the molars, will be compared to other known samples from that same time period. Many cultures practiced tooth modification such as tooth filing, as a sign of tribal affiliation and beauty. The pattern of the filing will be compared with patterns from existing African groups to determine who the individuals buried in the African Burial Ground are most closely related to.

The second goal is to look at the kinds of stress that these individuals faced throughout their lives. Already researchers have found that physical labor affected the skeletal structure in such a way that some female skeletons have the male attributes of large bones and muscle attachments. Cases of bone-scarring tuberculosis and syphilis, which were rare in Africa but prevalent in the colonial United States, show difficult adjustment and acculturation to Western diseases.

The data being collected on the burials will provide an important baseline that can be used to compare hypotheses about the spread of diseases, such as hypertension, in today's African-American community. It will also yield information on the levels of toxins in people living in America before the Industrial

Revolution and will help answer questions about the levels of toxins in our bodies today.

The last goal is to look at what kinds of cultural adaptations were occurring within the population that would have made adjustment to a new country and way of life easier. Artifacts such as shroud pins, glass beads, and cowrie shells and grave placement suggest religious beliefs. Graves facing east suggest Moslem burials, whereas graves facing west are typical of Christian burials. The community that the burial ground represents was poor, and there are few artifacts to study, but their placement and the individuals they are found with offer a unique opportunity to better understand the biology, health, and culture of the first generation of Africans living in this country, the ancestors of African Americans today.

Lone Survivor

It is rare to find a sample as large as 400 individuals; most archaeologists are lucky to find one. Skeletons, although they are sturdy and hard, are crushed under the movement of the earth and unknowingly destroyed by the living. But sometimes an almost perfect skeleton is uncovered. One such case involved forensic expert Rainer Henn of the Innsbruck Forensic Institute, whose job was to collect the bodies of hikers and mountain climbers lost in the Alps. Every spring the melting snow reveals the remains of unfortunate hikers who lost their life the previous winter. On September 23, 1991, a report on Henn's desk documented the sixth body found that year. The first two were mountain guides who disappeared in 1953, the third, a guide who lost his way in 1981, and the last two were hikers who had been reported missing in 1934—so old bodies were nothing new, but the sixth body, found on September 19, proved to be different. It was dark and leathery and fully preserved by natural freeze-drying affects of the wind and cold. It took 30 men using pickaxes and compressors to free the man from the ice. Once free, Henn realized that this man was special. Anthropologists determined that the man in the ice had been frozen for more than 5,000 years.

The Iceman, as he has been called, is kept in the University of Innsbruck's forensic lab deep freeze at −6° centigrade, the same temperature as the glacier that preserved him for so long. He is swaddled in layers of surgical gauze, sterilized crushed ice, and plastic, silently waiting for the international teams of scientists who will use the latest technology to find out who he was.

The Iceman's skin is hard. It takes a saw, not a scalpel, to cut off a small piece of tissue for analysis. Scientists are reluctant to cut into a body that is so rare, so X rays and CAT scans are used. X rays of the head revealed the sutures in the skull, which gave an age estimate of 35 to 40 years. The Iceman once stood 5 feet 3 inches tall, weighed only 110 pounds, and had dark hair and a full beard. But what did he look like? By using a CAT scan of the Iceman's head, scientists have created an exact copy of his skull. A model is made by passing an ultraviolet laser beam over the surface of a vat of photosensitive liquid plastic, which quickly hardens under the beam. The CAT scan images dictate where the laser is directed and, after each pass of the laser beam, the mass of hardened plastic is sunk deeper into the vat, gradually taking on a three-dimensional form one slice at a time. The skull model will be used to reconstruct the Iceman's face, which was partially destroyed from the movement of the glacier.

Already, scientists know a lot about the Iceman. His teeth were cavity free but worn down by the grinding action of eating a gritty diet of course-ground grain. A grooved earlobe suggests he wore an earring, and a series of strange tattoos that were found on the top of the left foot, across the knee cap, and running down the small of his back may have been placed there as some sort of folk medicine. Many cultures today place similar black-lined tattoos on parts of the body that ache, believing that they will cure the ailment. To test this hypothesis, X rays were taken of the Iceman's spine, knee, ankles, and feet. The X rays showed signs of degenerative wear and tear that might have been painful, so it seems reasonable to suggest that the Iceman placed tattoos on those spots believing they would heal the pain.

Earlier in his life, the Iceman had broken five ribs, which all healed well, but just before he died, his left arm was broken above the elbow and four ribs were cracked. From the bones, scientists have been able to reconstruct his last days. The man had probably gotten lost or caught in a storm and fell, breaking his ribs and arm. He found shelter in a depression of ice that kept him from the chilling winds. The Iceman laid down on his left side, off of his broken ribs, with his left arm extended. There, he froze to death, keeping his secrets for 5,000 years.

13

GIVING VOICE TO THE VICTIMS

*F*orensic scientists are often called to investigate deaths that have greater implications beyond the individual victim's tragedy. Government-sponsored terrorism results in thousands of deaths and one of the greatest roles the forensic anthropologist can play may be to investigate human-rights abuses, thus giving voice to the victims who dared to oppose their government.

Argentina

The political climate in Argentina in the mid-1970s was unstable. Although Isabel Perón, the third wife of beloved leader Juan Perón, was president she was unable to make needed social and econonic improvements. Radical leftist groups, made up of mostly college students, fought against the government and each other for political control. Leftist groups, including radical Peronists and the Montoneros, bombed government buildings as squads of soldiers and civilians patrolled the streets armed with assault rifles.

In 1976, the military seized power from Isabel Perón and set up a three-man military regime or junta on the pretext of leading the country back to democracy. But there was nothing democratic about the junta. It abolished the Congress, all labor unions, and political parties. Speaking out against the government became punishable by imprisonment and death. During the seven years that the junta held power, more than 10,000 people were killed at the hands of police death squads.

Armed police raided homes in the middle of the night, shooting people in their pajamas, or arresting them to be taken to secret detention camps. There, they were horribly tortured, often in front of spouses, parents, and children. Whole families were taken and never heard from again. Pregnant women who gave birth in prison never saw their babies, who were given to military families or sold for adoption. Mothers and grandmothers became very vocal about their missing children. They wanted answers, but the government ignored them and retaliated against them as well.

The largest group to suffer were the young college students who were members of the banned political parties. Sometimes the only "crime" they committed was socializing with someone thought to be a political activist.

Cristina Costanzo had been abducted at gunpoint early in the morning on October 14, 1976. In similar raids around the city, seven of her friends were also abducted and shoved into the black Fords that patrolled the streets collecting "political prisoners." Years later, Cristina's family learned that she had been put in prison that night, but her friends were not. The day after the abduction, seven bodies were found in a heap at the side of a dirt road at the edge of the city. Each had been shot once in the back of the head. These bodies were taken to the morgue and registered as N.N.—no name. Later that day they were piled on a truck along with other dead, taken to a cemetery, and buried in a mass grave similar to many others all over the country.

The bloody military reign ended in 1983, when the Argentine government, defeated by the British in the war over the Falkland Islands (Malvinas), disbanded and declared free elections. In 1984,

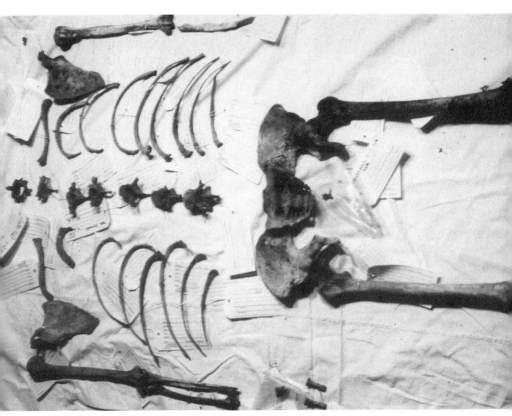

The bones of a victim are laid out in anatomical order ready for examination. (Kathleen O. Arries)

efforts were under way to identify the dead. Argentinians clambered for information about their missing relatives who became known as "the disappeared," but most of the disappeared had been buried in mass graves, registered only as N.N.

Forensic anthropologist Clyde Snow along with a group of anthropology students from Argentina University showed the world how forensic identification methods could give mourning families a little peace. He taught students how to judge sex, race, and age from bones and help piece together broken lives like those of the Costanzo family.

In 1984 when the cemetery was opened, many bodies were uncovered, and put in plastic bags to be taken to the morgue and identified by Clyde Snow and Lowell Levine, a forensic odontologist who perfected the techniques of identifying the dead through dental X rays. At the morgue, Snow and Levine were shown into a small room lined with plastic garbage bags full of bones. Broken bags spilled out their contents on the dirty floor, where no one had bothered to pick them up.

Only one family had sent in information to help in identifying the remains. The Costanzos sent in dental X rays taken one year before Cristina disappeared. Levine looked at the X ray as Snow started to open the bags and pull out skulls. He lined them up on the long examining tables, grouping them by sex and age. They were interested in the group of skulls 20–30 years old. Cristina was 25. Most of the skulls had gunshot wounds in them, some in the back of the head in a typical execution style. Snow fingered one skull that seemed to fit Cristina's description, but several teeth had been lost from the upper row during the exhumation. Fortunately the lower jaw was intact and could be x-rayed. Placing the two X rays side by side, Levine showed Snow that the fillings were a perfect match, the root shapes, and bone pattern were identical. It was Cristina Costanzo.

Because of Snow's efforts, Argentina has the only national forensic anthropology team in the world. It has identified hundreds of bodies and relieved many families' doubts about the fate of their children. Many people ask why try to do the impossible? Why try to identify the thousands of disappeared? But those doing the work say that they need to show governments that they will be held accountable for their crimes. Through forensic investigation, the crimes have been documented and proved in a court of law. Snow himself has testified in court, showing slides of the shattered skulls, the bullet holes, and then the photographs of the young men and woman the bones represented.

Hungary

Similar recovery efforts have taken place in Hungary more than 30 years after the Hungarian revolution of October 1956. The revolt started out as a demonstration by the students of Budapest's

Technological University. Students marched down the main street of Budapest, the capital of Hungary, and over the bridge that crossed the Danube River. But the demonstration quickly escalated to an armed fight by the Hungarian citizens to oust the Soviet Union, which had occupied the country and controlled its economy since the end of World War II. The revolution lasted a euphoric 12 days in which it appeared that Soviet forces were leaving the country, but they returned with reinforcements and retaliated with a vengeance. On November 4, the Soviet army invaded Budapest and by evening most of the buildings suffered gaping holes from tank fire. Thousands of civilians were shot as the tanks rolled through the streets.

To defuse the revolt, the Hungarian government picked up known radical organizers and imprisoned them with others who had been arrested months before for speaking out against Soviet-imposed communism. As the prisons filled, prisoners were executed and dumped in mass, unmarked graves.

Thirty-four years later in 1990, after the Iron Curtain fell, Hungary like Argentina was ready to have the atrocities of war documented and the dead identified. Michael Finnegan spent time in Hungary reviewing the cases of the disappeared at the National Museum of Hungary. For each case, the Hungarian scientific team collected as much information as they could about those individuals who were suspected of having died in prison in the 1950s. Old photographs, medical records, and interviews with relatives were compared with the skeletal data. The work in Hungary is difficult because the information is not readily available. When some of the mass graves were uncovered, workers found small aluminum tags tied to feet. These tags were inscribed with a number, which suggests the existence of a master list, a log of those who were buried. But the government officials, many of whom are still in power, are not eager to dredge up their past involvement and risk retribution, but slowly, the information is coming to light. Hungary is eager to know the truth, but unlike Argentina prosecution for those involved is not likely. When all the bodies have been identified then the chaos of 1956 will truly be history.

Casualties of War

In Vietnam, folklore says that having the bones of an American soldier is the golden passport through U.S. immigration and worth money. So some Vietnamese farmers who come across human bones often scoop them up and take them in to get a reward. But the U.S. Army does not pay for bones, and bones separated from the clothing and artifacts are more difficult to identify. The best results occur when U.S. search teams go in and look for plane crashes and battle sites. Like any other forensic case, the site is excavated and the remains are taken back to be examined.

In June 1974, a group of Vietnamese woodcutters walked out of the heavily wooded area they had been working in with eight cassette tapes and a microphone they had recovered from the wreckage of a plane. The tapes were delivered to the U.S. Army, who listened to the tapes and concluded that the plane the wood-cutters found along with the crew were American. But at the time, the army was flooded with recovery jobs so they sent the woodcutters back into the jungle to get more information and take pictures. Five days later, the woodcutters arrived with Polaroid pictures of the plane, aircraft parts, a notebook, three handguns, three hunting knives, and a map of the area. The personal effects revealed that one American and two Vietnamese victims had died in the crash. The Vietnamese and American governments wanted the proper remains returned to them.

A team was sent in to collect the remains, which were then temporarily housed in the Army of the Republic of Viet Nam Military Hospital in Saigon, unceremoniously wrapped in four plastic bags. Charles Warren, the anthropologist assigned to the case, was dismayed to find out that the bones were jumbled, and all identifying tags and clothing had been removed, making his job much harder since he could not easily assign a BTB (believed to be) label to any of them.

Because of the extreme heat and humidity of the area where the bones were found, the ends of the long bones had eroded, which would hinder reassembling the skeletons. Also, many of the major

∇

parts of the skeletons were missing. There were three skulls—one with a broken jawbone, one minus the occipital bone, and one with a shattered face. Examining the facial features, Warren picked out the American's skull based on the caucasoid narrow nasal opening and prominent cheekbones. One of the skulls was definitely Asian, but the other with the shattered face could not be positively identified. There was no other information to go on and no medical records to compare the skeletons to. The Vietnamese remains were returned to the Vietnamese government, and the American remains were sent to the Central Identification Lab in Hawaii, for further examination.

In the 1990s, the U.S. Army still conducts search and recovery operations to locate dead American soldiers from the Vietnam War, the Korean War, and World Wars I and II. Just recently a B22 bomber plane was found in the jungle of New Guinea and efforts are being made to identify the crew. Soldiers from the War of 1812 who were found in Canadian soil are ceremoniously returned to the United States with all of the pomp and circumstance due any soldier. Soldiers are not the only ones identified in the various recovery efforts, civilians such as missionaries who were captured and died in captivity and news correspondents and camera crews who had been ambushed have also been recovered and sent back to their homelands.

The Homeless

Political victims are only one kind of victim. Another are the homeless in the United States who roam the streets and alleyways looking for a warm place to rest. They are not the disappeared but the invisible, the people who fall between the cracks of bureaucracy.

Douglas Ubelaker remembered one man who was found frozen to death under a bridge. An electrical fire along a system of cables in the bridge construction led police to a crawl space. As they pulled out the burned cables they pulled out bones as well. Many homeless people have found shelter under bridges and inside crawl spaces, anywhere where they can find some warmth. If it hadn't been for the fire, no one ever would have found him. This man had apparently died several years earlier because he was completely skeletonized.

As Ubelaker examined the bones, he was able to piece together the man's life. In his youth the man had been robust and healthy. His teeth showed signs of good dental care as a child, a good indication that he once had a family who loved and cared for him, but more recent trauma revealed his adult life had been harsh. His face and other parts of his body showed signs of violent physical abuse and malnutrition. Tooth decay and abscesses in the roots and gums would have caused a lot of pain. Alone and in pain, this man froze to death in the only shelter he could find, under a bridge that a city full of people crossed everyday.

Douglas Ubelaker believes that using science to give the homeless a last chance to tell us who they were and what happened to them is one of the most important contributions forensic anthropologists make: "We are the spokesperson for the dead, their last chance to get their message out."

Silent Witness

Although forensic anthropologists work with the dead, their work has significance for the living too. Computer superimposition, for example, is being used to find missing children, by "aging" a photograph of a missing child to get an image of what the child might look like two, five, or 10 years later. The photo can be circulated throughout the country years after the child's disappearance in the hope that someone might notice a resemblance and identify the child.

To the living, the use of forensics can establish innocence as well as guilt. No longer does it matter if someone looks like a criminal or is in the wrong place at the wrong time as in Cesare Lombroso's day. With DNA testing if someone is innocent, forensics may prove it.

∇

The Future

In the future, chemical analysis will become routine as it becomes less costly and more widely available to law enforcement. DNA analysis may become the standard method for identifying otherwise unidentifiable bodies. Testing for trace elements such as strontium 87 will enable scientists to determine the origin of a body, and the amount of strontium 87 and 86 found in individual bones will be used to more easily segregate the bones of many people found at a crime or accident site.

Research scientists continue to push the field of forensic anthropology toward more accurate time-of-death estimates and recognition of the subtle signs that indicate murder. Bones last a long time, longer than other types of evidence such as clothing, blood stains, and footprints. They even outlast the murderers themselves, and for those scientists who are trained to hear, these bones speak loudly. As Clyde Snow is fond of saying, "Bones make good witnesses, they never lie and they never forget."

GLOSSARY

Terms in the glossary appear in *italics* the first time they are used in the text. They may not always appear exactly as listed here.

adipocere A waxy white material that is formed when body fat decays in the presence of moisture.

anthropology The study of humans, their cultures, and societies.

anthropometry The study of human body measurements.

archaeological excavation The process of uncovering past cultures by digging systematically for artifacts.

articulation The point where two adjacent bones are joined together.

autolysis The natural process of decomposition where the enzymes in a corpse digest the body.

cortex The hard, dense outer layer of bone.

cranial suture The seam where two bones of the skull meet and fuse together.

diaphysis The shaft of the long bones.

epiphysis The joint end of the long bones.

exhume To dig out of the earth.

facial reconstruction The process of molding a clay face on to a skull.

forensic A legal argument or procedures that can be used in a court of law.

forensic entomology The study of insects to help solve criminal cases.

forensic odontologists Scientists who study the teeth and dental work of dead individuals in order to establish the identity of the victims.

green bone Bone that is less than one year old and has a greasy feel to it.

long bone The bones of the arms and legs; humerus, radius, ulna, femur, tibia, and fibula.

ossification The natural process of the formation and hardening of the bones.

osteometric board A tool for measuring the length of the long bones.

osteons Circular tunnels within the bone that hold blood vessels and nerve fibers.

perimortem Before death.

phalanges Finger and toe bones.

physical anthropology The science of the human body; its evolution, adaptation to the environment and its diversity.

postmortem After death.

putrefaction The natural process of decomposition where bacteria in a dead body continue to reproduce and feed.

repatriate To return the remains of dead men and women to their homelands.

superimposition A photographic technique that places a photo of a skull over a portrait of a person in order to compare skeletal and facial features.

FURTHER READING

Cohen, Sharron. *Mysteries of Research*. Fort Atkinson, Wis.: Highsmith Press, 1992. A paperback book that explains the types of criminal research in anthropology, archaeology, and sociology.

Joyce, Christopher, and Eric Stover. *Witnesses from the Grave: The Stories Bones Tell*. Boston: Little, Brown, 1991. An in-depth history of forensic anthropology and a fascinating account of Clyde Snow's groundbreaking career.

Larsen, Anita. *True Crimes and How They Were Solved*. New York: Scholastic, 1993. A small paperback that highlights actual crimes and how they were solved by forensic ballistics, entomology, and fingerprinting.

Schwartz, Jeffrey H. *What the Bones Tell Us*. New York: Henry Holt and Co., 1993. A brief discussion of bone analysis followed by an in-depth study of Neandertal remains.

Spindler, Konrad. *The Man in the Ice*. London: Weidenfeld and Nicolson, 1993. This book chronicles the discovery of the Iceman and includes a technical discussion of the testing conducted on it and what researchers have found thus far.

Tesar, Jenny. *Scientific Crime Investigation*. New York: Watts, 1991. An introduction to forensic lab techniques, including fingerprinting, autopsies, and polygraph testing.

Ubelaker, Douglas and Henry Scammell. *Bones: A Forensic Detective's Casebook*. New York: HarperCollins, 1992. An extensive look at the cases that have crossed the desk of Smithsonian curator Ubelaker. It also includes technical information and historical background.

INDEX

Italic numbers indicate illustrations.

A
adipocere   34, 36
African Burial Ground (New York)   116–118
age determination   15, *48*, 48–51
    children   *49*, 50–51
    Mengele, Josef   99
American Association of Forensic Anthropology   15
American Museum of Natural History (New York)   89
Andres, Peter   70
Angel, Lawrence   16, 58, 68
animal bones
    bear   *17*, 19–21, *20*
    bird   *18*, 19
    chicken   68–69
    compared to human   16–22, *17, 18*
    deer   *17*
    dog   *17*, 19, 22
    horse   *17*, 21–22
animal teeth marks   70, 113–114
anthropometry   10–11
archaeological excavation   *24*, 24–25
archaeological sites
    African Burial Ground   116–118
    laws pertaining to   114
    Native American   112, 113
    Neandertal   107
Argentina   121–124
Army, United States   15
Arries, Kathleen O.   17–18, 24–26, 79–82

Australopithicus robustus   110
autolysis   35

B
Barnes, Jeffery   37
Bass, Dr. William M.
    forensic response team   29, 30
    race determination   53
    TARF   31–35, *32*
bear bones   *17*, 19–21, *20*
Bertillon, Alphonse   10, 11
blackfly   41
blowfly   37, *38*, 39
bones
    cleaning   30
    composition   19, 67
    cross section   *18*
    ossification   *48*, 47–50
Boyer, Mitch   93, *94*, 95
Branch Davidian Cult incident   73
buried remains   26–*28*, 33, 36
burned bone   73–76
    reconstruction of   *75, 76*

C
C. A. Pound Human Identification Lab   65, 92
Case Western Reserve Medical School   12
Cassidy, Butch   103–106, *105*
CAT scan (computerized axial tomography)   109, 119
caucasoid race   52–53, 77, 80, 81
chemical analysis   61, 109–110, 129

Chicago Medical College   4
Chicago, University of   2
chicken bones   68–69
climate
    decomposition   35–37
    insects   39–40
computer superimposition   96, 128
coroner   9. *See also* medical examiner
cranial sutures   *viii*, 49

D

decay rate   32–36
dental remains
    health status   62, 128
    Mengele, Josef   101
    Parkman, Dr. George   7
    positive identification   24, 63, 124
    repatriation   15
diaphyses   19, *46*
"disappeared"   123
disease   60–62
    archaeology   111–112, 117
DNA (deoxyribonucleic acid)   63, *64*,
    65, 106, 117, 129
    decomposition   34
dog training   34
Dorsey, Dr. George   *3*, 4–5
Dwight, Dr. Thomas   11, 54

E

Earhart, Amelia   101–102
Egyptian remains   *108*, 108–109, 111,
    112
ELISA (enzyme-linked immunosorbent
    assay)   111
epiphyses   16, 19, 47, *48*
Erie Community College   17
ethics   103, 114–115
Evers, Medgar   103

F

facial reconstruction   77–89
    early humans   89
    "Frank"   79–82
    "Grinner"   83, *84–88*
    His, Wilhelm   77–78
    Iceman   119

FBI (Federal Bureau of Investigation)
    11–13, 21, 22, 34, 96
fiberoptic endoscope   109
Field Museum of Natural History (Chi-
    cago)   4
fingerprints   10–11, 29, 62
Finnegan, Dr. Michael   30, 59, 70–72,
    125
Florida, University of   65, 92
forensic
    definition   4
    entomology   37–38, 41
    odontology   63, 123–124
    research   13–15, 31–35, 68–69
Fram, Robert   13

G

Gacy, John Wayne   83
Gatliff, Betty Pat   82–83
genetic fingerprinting.   *See* DNA
George Washington University   102
Gleser, G. C.   54, 55
green bone   36
gunshot trauma   33, 66–67

H

handedness   58–59, 99
Harvard Medical School   6, 7
Harvard University   11
height.   *See* stature determination
Helmer, Richard   98–100
Henn, Rainer   118
His, Wilhelm   77–78
Hoffman, Michael   20
Hole in the Wall Gang   *105*
Holmes, Oliver Wendell   7
homeless   127–128
horse bones   *17*, 21–22
Howard University (Washington, D.C.)
    117
human-rights abuse
    Argentina   121–124
    Hungary   124–125
    Hungarian revolution   124–125

I

Iceman   118–120

Innsbruck Forensic Institute   118
insects   35, 37–41
isotopes   110

K
Kansas State University   30
Keep, Nathan   7
Kerley, Ellis   51, 99
knife trauma   68–69, *72*, 73
Korean War dead   15, 54
Koresh, David   73
Krogman, Wilton M.   12

L
larvae   35, 37, *38*, 39–41
lead poisoning   110
Levine, Lowell   123–124
Lewis, Meriwether   102
Lindow Man   *115*, 115–116
Littlefield, Ephraim   6–7, 8
Lombroso, Cesare   10, 128
Long, Huey   102
Luetgert, Adolphe   1–5

M
Maples, Dr. William   65, 92, 95–96
McKern, Thomas   50
medical examiner   9, 21, 29, 30
medical technology   108–109
Mengele, Josef   97–101, *100*
mongoloid race   52, 53, 80, 81
mummy.   *See* Egyptian remains
muscle attachments   44, 46, 58, 117

N
National Museum of Natural History at
    the Smithsonian Institution (Washing-
    ton, D.C.)   16, 21, 27, 36, 66, 68, 73
    FBI   11–12, *13*
    skeletal collection   11, *12*, 114
Native American Graves Protection and
    Repatriation Act   114
Native American remains   112, 113–115
natural disasters   28–29
Natural History Museum (London)   70
Neandertal remains   107
negroid race   52–53, 80, 81

New York State Museum (Albany)   37,
    89

O
occupational trauma   57–58, 61, 108,
    117
ossification   *48*, 48–50
osteometric board   *54*, 55
osteons   19, 22, 51
Owsley, Douglas   27, 66

P
paleoanthropology   89, 107–108
Parkman, Dr. George   5–8
pelvis
    age indicators   50
    sexual differences   *43*, 44
perimortem trauma   67
phalanges   20, 21
photographic superimposition   90–96,
    91, 92
    Boyer, Mitch   93–95, *94*
    Butch and Sundance   106
    Mengele, Josef   99–100
physical anthropology   4, 11, 108
postmortem trauma   67
pubic symphysis   *43*, 44, 46, 50
putrefaction   35

R
race indicators   51–53, 94, 127
    reconstruction   80, 81
radiograph   95, 109
repatriation   15, 126–127

S
sex determination   4, 42–48
    Mengele, Josef   99
    pelvis   *43*, 44
    skull   *45*, 47
sinus print   62–63
skeleton, human   *vii*, 42
skull   *viii*
    age indicators   49–50
    race indicators   52–53
    reconstruction   77–89
    sexual differences   *45*, 47

superimposition   90–95, 92, 96, 99–
   100, 106
Smithsonian.   *See* National Museum of
   Natural History at the Smithsonian Institution
Snow, Clyde   83, 129
   Butch and Sundance case   103–106
   Josef Mengele case   98
   Mitch Boyer case   93–95
   work in Argentina   123–124
soil   27, 36
Southern Institute of Forensic Science
   74
Starrs, James   102, 103
stature determination   8, 11, 14, 15, 54–
   55, 74, 99
Stewart, T. Dale   12, 15, 21–22, 50
strangulation   25
strontium   110, 129
Sundance Kid   103–106, *105*
superimposition.   *See* photographic superimposition

T

TARF (Tennessee Anthropological Research Facility)   31–35
teeth   33–34. *See also* dental remains
   age indicator   *50*, 50–51
   filing   117
   occupational trauma   57–58
   superimposition   92
Tennessee fireworks explosion   30
Tennessee, University of   29, 31
time of death   8, 31–41
   insect data   37–41
   rate of decay   34–37
   research   31–34
Todd, T. Wingate   50
trace elements   109–110, 129
Trotter, Mildred   15, 54, 55

U

Ubelaker, Douglas
   animal bones   22
   Branch Davidian case   73
   chicken bone experiment   68–69
   FBI   13
   homeless   127–128

V

Vietnam War remains   126–127
Vucetich, Juan   10–11

W

Waldrip, Edward, Ph.D.   74, *75*
Warren, Charles   126–127
Washington University (St. Louis)   15
weapons   70–73
   knives   68–69, *72*, 113
   tools   *71*, 72–73
Webster, Dr. John   6–8
Weiss, Carl   102
Wiesenthal Center   98, 101
World War II remains   14–15, 54, 127
wounds, skeletal   66–67, *71, 72,* 73, 113,
   116
Wymans, Jefferies   7

X

X-rays   56, 67, 95, 99, 109
   dental   124
   Egyptian   *108*
   Iceman   119
   sinus   62–63

Y

Y-chromosome fluorescence   46–47